#MMENTS

#MMENTS

A Collection of Stories About
the NBA and Twitter, Told by a
Guy Who's Addicted to Both

THANE JACKSON

ARTWORK BY: KATIE STEERE
EDITED BY: DANIEL McCURRY

Contents

For my wife, who has supported this goal
and my love of basketball both willingly and
sometimes begrudgingly from day one.

For both of my parents, who taught me that I
could do anything I set my mind too, including
writing this extremely silly and ridiculous book.

For Damian Lillard and the Portland Trail
Blazers, for everything we've been through.

And finally, for everyone who thinks I spend
too much time talking about basketball,
watching basketball, or checking my Twitter
feed. This is for all of you as well.

#

I Remember That
Day on Twitter

THE INSPIRATION FOR THIS BOOK WAS THE way many millennials gain inspiration for just about anything--a lively and drunken conversation aided by smartphone fact-checking to call people out on their bullshit.

It was the summer of 2017 and whatever *ESPN* program was on at the bar was doing one of those "on this date" segments. This one featured Kevin Durant making everyone at Harlem's famed Rucker Park question their manhood by dropping 66 points in a pick-up game. Durant was hardly the first NBA player to stop by for a quick game at Rucker - others include Kobe Bryant, Wilt Chamberlain, Stephon Marbury, and Kareem Abdul-Jabbar, and he certainly won't be the last.[1] However, this appearance was slightly different from any other cameo at the playground haven.

---

1   My favorites to ever cross the Rucker lines are Earl "Black Jesus" Monroe (More commonly known as "The Pearl" but his street

We were absentmindedly watching the television when a buddy of mine piped up: "I remember that day on Twitter." The whole table seemed put off by this comment, but I couldn't help but think the same thing. I remember watching the whole thing about Durant on my Twitter feed, something I hadn't done before. To say that he went bonkers on these dudes is probably an understatement. He was pulling up from damn near half-court, and draining treys left and right, four in a row to end the game. All the while, he was snatching rebounds out of the sky and not playing any semblance of defense, because he knew he didn't have to. He'd knock down a shot right in some dude's grill, and then celebrate with his boys in the stands, as everyone began to spill onto the court. He'd head back just in time to get the rebound, bring the ball back up the court, and do it all over again[2]. It was incredible, and I felt like I was there for it.

I mean, I wasn't *really* there, but I was there. In the stands, I swear. Right there with everyone else following every tiny Twitter reaction and shitty camera

---

name was Black Jesus, so for this section that's what I'm using), Jumpin Jackie Jackson, Pee Wee Kirkland and Nate "Tiny" Archibald. Basically, only guys with great nicknames played in Harlem.

2   Yes, I'm aware this pickup game was against (to put it nicely) players that lacked NBA talent. Still, it was a difficult thing to do, considering the double park rims and a full crowd spilling onto the court.

#M🏀MENTS

phone video that was posted while KD was putting on his show. At least, it felt that way as I followed.

This is why Twitter and the NBA belong in the same book. These two things were *made* for each other. Durant's Rucker explosion happened during the 2011 NBA lockout, when hoops junkies like me were desperate for anything to quench our thirst for our favorite players getting buckets at the expense of mere mortals. Perhaps coincidentally, Twitter surpassed 100 million monthly users right around the time everyone was reacting to Durant's outburst - more than doubling its numbers from the year prior. The span of reactions during this pick-up game made the basketball world smaller for a brief moment and brought fans closer to an NBA superstar than ever before. #NBATwitter was officially born, an inclusive community without an actual location, but which is constantly evolving. Here, teams, executives, players (current and retired), fans, and league officials all gather in one virtual place to yell at each other and respond to whatever is happening. Billions of individuals, reacting all at once.

Basketball itself is a game of reactions: five people moving simultaneously in response to rapidly unfolding events. Their reactions - whether correct, incorrect, or indifferent - spur other reactions, and the game keeps moving while the ball is in play. The beautiful thing is that all that activity spurs equally kinetic reactions from #NBATwitter as well. Sometimes it's boring, other times it's all sorts of bizarre chaos. Even better, the NBA players who cause these reactions in the first place, often now log on and interact with the rest of the world regarding the events taking place. #NBATwitter has changed the league into a reality television show, and we just can't help piling onto one moment after another.

#

I need to thank Shea Serrano for giving me direction for this book. One of the things Shea is great at - and one of the reasons he is someone I look up to, is if you ask for feedback, he'll give it to you. I emailed him once to tell him I wanted to write a book about the relationship between the NBA and social media, without really knowing what to do with it. He said that "It sounds more like an article than a 250-page book or whatever. If you really want to do this, then you have to figure out what it is before you start."

At first, I was a little hurt that the author of a book[3] I thoroughly enjoyed wasn't super on-board with my thoughts. Especially since he was a successful writer and I was pretty much a real-life Jim Halpert. However, after thinking about it, I decided he was right. That's when my idea started to grow into its current form: a collection of stories about Twitter

---

3   Basketball (And Other Things)

and the NBA. It's not about the games, that's an important distinction. Rather, it's about the fleeting moments that had all of us staring at Twitter on our phones, waiting for the next reaction.

I didn't want this book to be a "History of Twitter" or a "History of the NBA". It will be a small amount of both, but to me that's not what it's *about*. Instead, I want this to be an entertaining and slightly ridiculous look at the league I love, along with some of the things that happen outside of basketball that make the NBA so much fun. Because that's what the NBA and Twitter both are, a freakin' blast. The NBA is the best reality television show on the planet, a wild mix of *The Bachelor,* The *Real World, American Ninja Warrior,* and *Iron Chef*[4]. We can't always watch the games, or be there, but Twitter is live all the time, literally allowing us to interact with each moment as it's happening. I love basketball - especially the NBA - and I love Twitter. Both are equally cool on their own, but this is sort of like a baseball and steroids thing. One is absolutely better with the other.

-TJ

---

4   I chose these particular television shows because they are equally competitive and ridiculous.

How Deandre Jordan Found Love

EVERY THURSDAY NIGHT IN THE SUMMER OF 2003, groups of teenagers got a ride from their parents to gather in their friends' homes to take part in a cultural phenomenon unlike any we had seen before. Let's take a quick tour of 2003. A gallon of gas averaged $1.83 per gallon, Saddam Hussein was found living in a hole in the ground, and instead of Twitter, Facebook, and Instagram teens and tweens were ranking their friends one through eight on Myspace, the original platform for sliding into someone's inbox uninvited.[5]

There was one place and one place only in which you could find everyone within your Top 8[6] and those clamoring to sneak into it, consistently gathering as

---

5   I'm just now realizing how screwed up it was that MySpace literally used to make us rank our friends numerically.

6   This isn't exactly true, I had Allen Iverson in my Myspace Top 8. You could pretty much put anyone there. Like I said, this was a really screwed up system.

one, and that was to take part in the borderline religious experience of viewing the new episode of *The O.C.*[7] One could consider this experience as the "original" #NBATwitter, a community reacting to the unnecessarily dramatic in probably the worst way possible. *The O.C.* spawned relationships as quickly as it destroyed them, both in our actual lives as well as those on the show. The most fascinating of those were the trials of the endlessly divided Seth Cohen.

When we're introduced to Seth, he almost immediately confesses his love for a girl named Summer Roberts, a commonly desired socialite and classmate at The Harbor School. The predictable problems at this point are that Seth had barely spoken to Summer and on the surface at least, they have no common ground or interests. As Season One progresses Seth and Summer are involved in the missteps of their best friends, Ryan and Marissa and it's at this point that we discover maybe, just maybe the apple of Seth's eye could perhaps grow to feel at least somewhat the same way as he does. Finally, just as it seems that Seth and Summer are about to potentially get off the ground, transfer student Anna Stern enters the story and throws everything off the rails.

Remember when I said that, on the surface Seth and Summer had nothing in common? To put it plainly Seth and Anna do not have that problem.

---

7   If you don't honestly believe The O.C. Is one of the greatest shows of all time, I'm not sure I can trust your judgment. I still tell my friends "Welcome to The O.C. Bitch!" on a semi-regular basis.

Much like Seth, Anna is smart, slightly dorky and despises her surroundings in the same general loathing way that Seth does. She enjoys three out of four of Seth's favorite pastimes in sailing, comic books, and witty banter. Unsurprisingly the two hit it off much to the chagrin of Summer who was beginning to enjoy Seth's attention. While (mostly) friends[8] Anna and Summer unwittingly duel for Seth's affection like LeBron and Steph duel for Larry O'Brien trophies[9] until Anna makes her move on New Year's Eve.

Seth initially began dating Anna for a short period of time, and why wouldn't he? She had everything he wanted in a girl, and Summer on numerous occasions made it clear she wasn't interested. Seth appeared committed for the long haul, although thoughts of what could have been and what could be with Summer were never far away. This reached its boiling point on a group trip where Summer, now on board with the long-term potential of the relationship, deployed the full court press often interrupting Seth and Anna's "alone time" and began displaying interest in comics. Anna seeing through this as an attempt

---

8   When it's discovered that both Anna and Summer have feelings for Seth, he doesn't know how to handle this and plays both for a while unbeknownst to the other (idiot). He spends Thanksgiving hiding each woman in a different part of the house and running back and forth between the two. They of course find out and make him choose, he chooses neither (double idiot) in an attempt to not hurt someone's feelings.

9   In this scenario Anna is LeBron and Summer is Steph. I'll stand on this hill forever.

to win Seth over, eventually does what Seth never has the stones to do. She makes a difficult decision, breaking up with Seth leaving him free to choose the woman he desired all along.

For Clippers and Mavs fans this story should sound all too familiar, two suitors both competing over an indecisive beau complete with the incumbent pulling out all the stops to win him back? That's #NBATwitter's favorite love-triangle/hostage situation story: DeAndre Jordan's 2015 free agency decision.

#

It all started with an emoji airplane. During the age of social media, we all know what this means. Literally anyone can post an emoji airplane and it means some version of the same thing. I'm coming. On my way. Wheels up. See you soon. This time was no different as all those things were indeed implied. However, there was one additional implication that, while perhaps unintended, sparked one of the more entertaining and confusing days in #NBATwitter history.

That message? Something is wrong, I'm going to fix it.

Back in May of 2015 the "Lob City" Clippers[10]

---

10   If you are interested in reading this book, I'm going to make the assumption that you know what I am referring to when I say Lob City. If you don't, go ahead and take some time to look it up. I can wait.

had just been eliminated by the underdog Houston Rockets in Game 7 of the Western Conference Semi-finals - after blowing a 3-1 series lead - before Golden State made doing such a thing cool. Part of Houston's successful comeback can be attributed to their strategy of intentionally fouling DeAndre Jordan and forcing him to shoot free throws,[11] thus prompting Clippers Coach Doc Rivers to pull Jordan from the game at important moments, rather than leave him in as a liability. There were reports after the series that Jordan and Clippers point guard Chris Paul were feuding after the loss regarding Jordan's work ethic, especially when it came to free throw shooting[12]. While Jordan and his trials and tribulations at the line weren't *really* the reason the Clippers blew the series, he was certainly an easy target for fans, teammates, and the media. It was a tough time for DeAndre. All he wanted was love, and he needed a friend. Enter Chandler Parsons of the Dallas Mavericks.

Every Seth Cohen needs a Ryan Atwood[13].

---

11 Jordan, a notoriously poor free-throw shooter shot just 39.7% during the 14-15 regular season. During the series against Houston he shot better, but still terrible. Around 46% including a horrid 14-34 in Game 4 of the series. For comparison, equally poor free-throw shooter Dwight Howard actually shot worse than Jordan during the same Western Conference Semis at 38%, but he got the win, so it's looked at way differently.

12 It's pretty well known that Chris Paul is a total prick. I like to imagine he acts like this toward his teammates because he's the least cool person in the Banana Boat Gang.

13 I hate this analogy, but it's what worked considering the role Parsons played in this whole story. Really, he's more of Marissa Cooper.

Someone to party with, someone to push him outside of his comfort zone, and someone to make him realize his worth and help him believe in himself. Sharing the same agent, Dan Fegan[14], Parsons and Jordan developed quite the bond partying for an entire week heading into free agency beginning on July 1st. They dined, went to clubs, and fell for each other much the same way Seth and Anna fell for each other. Jordan simply wanted to be appreciated and not be a third wheel. Parsons was aching for a partner in crime. As soon as Jordan was free of his contractual obligations to the Clippers, Mav's owner Mark Cuban came storming in to seal the deal and capitalize on Parsons' flirtation. Two days later after more parties and extravagant meals, the wildly impulsive[15] DeAndre Jordan committed to a four-year $80 million deal with the Mavericks, hinging on a pitch centered on him being a focal point of the offense and the centerpiece of the franchise. No more living in Chris Paul's shadow.

That was that, it was done. Until five days later Mark Stein of ESPN dropped a bomb. Jordan was having second thoughts about signing with Dallas,

---

14 It should be noted that Fegan and Mavericks owner Mark Cuban are pretty tight, much to the chagrin of the rest of the NBA who scream foul play anytime a Fegan client is in contact with Dallas.

15 Yes, I'm mostly assuming this, but there are stories of DJ buying cars and returning them a month later. By the 2015 season he was also on his third different agent, at the time of writing this he is on his fourth.

#M●MENTS

and the Clippers were now trying to don a Wonder Woman outfit and win him back.[16]

The NBA is the best league on the planet, but not without its faults. The glaring hole in the entire business is that almost all "official" business during the offseason is done during a time when none of it can actually be made official. Unlike other major professional sports, the NBA's business moratorium allows free agency deals to be agreed to; however, they cannot actually be signed and made official until the moratorium has ended, which was July 9th, seven full days after Jordan had agreed to join Dallas[17]. This obviously creates a bit of a handshake agreement that no funny business will take place once things have been agreed on, but that isn't always the case, and it does give players time to change their minds[18].

The league being full of dramatic, impulsive people that are very much nocturnal, no one really believes that business isn't "done" before the moratorium period begins at 12AM on the first of July, with many deals being announced almost the minute that free agency begins. This isn't exactly a merry band of

16   Don't worry, we will get to this.

17   Jordan agreed to a contract with Dallas on July 3rd, 2015, he could not officially sign it until 12AM on July 9th.

18   In 2009 Hedo Turkoglu agreed to a deal with my beloved Trail Blazers only to back out and agree with Toronto about a day later. That same season Elton Brand backed out of a deal with Atlanta. More recently Nemanja Bjelica had agreed to a deal with the 76ers, only to back out claiming he was going to play in Europe, only to back out of that to sign with the Sacramento Kings.

thieves; however, this is clearly a bit of a loophole in the system. Think of it like college athletes verbally agreeing to a school then not being able to actually sign there for a while. Those guys back out of deals all the time, so it's only natural to think that someone could possibly get to a young and impressionable player and sway his thinking. So, when Mark Stein tweeted at 12PM the day before the 2015 moratorium period ended, the NBA world knew shit was clearly about to hit the fan.

What happened over the next 12 or so hours was Twitter madness. Cue Chandler Parsons music again and the emoji airplane that caused a fairly straightforward situation to tumble into utter disarray. Word was that the Clippers saw an opening with Jordan's subtle signal of distress (via the Stein tweet) and were converging upon Jordan's home in Houston, where he had returned for the offseason. NBA players are nothing if not showmen. So, when it looked like Parsons[19] was coming to save the day with his small but impactful Twitter post, Jordan's current/ex/soon to be current

---

19   It should be noted that I'm not sure if Parsons ever actually went to Houston. In interviews after that night Parsons and Mark Cuban both stated something to the effect of, Parsons went to LA in case DJ was there and Cuban went to Houston. This was semi-confirmed when ESPN's Chris Broussard made a statement that Cuban was going crazy and driving around Houston aimlessly searching for Jordan's house. Cuban later called Broussard a liar and said he never left his hotel. Bottom line here, Cuban was in Houston, and Parsons was never confirmed to be in the city.

#M●MENTS

Clipper teammates (many of whom were already in Houston or nearby) got into the action as well.

It started with JJ Redick who, being the nearest in Austin, Texas, sent an emoji of a car. Blake Griffin, who had replaced Parsons as DJ's dinner companion the night before, went over-the-top dramatic-and very on brand for this day in #NBATwitter history-choosing to post three different vehicles in one Tweet. A car, a plane to match Parsons, and to top it off a helicopter. Even the vacationing Chris Paul was brought into action from his "bro"-cation with LeBron, Carmelo Anthony, and Dwayne Wade[20] to capsize his feud with Jordan and tow him back to Los Angeles with a series of emojis that clearly meant banana boat. Others got in the act as well. Clippers assistant coaches thought it would be fun to post emojis representing other forms of travel.[21] Some certain shoe brands displayed their perceived greatness in emoji format, teams' individual social media crews reminded everyone paying attention about the accolades their club had accumulated (basically accounts without any sort of investment in what was actually going on kept chiming in with their own emojis, which is pretty much #NBATwitter in a nutshell). However, hands down the top moment of the day came from

---

20   This is another one of those "if you have an interest in this book, I'm assuming you know about…" moments. I could probably write an entire chapter on the Banana Boat Crew honestly.

21   Mike Woodson indicated that he would swim to the meeting.

Paul Pierce, who proved that he didn't know how to use a smartphone, or an emoji, by posting a clipart picture of a rocket ship emoji - rather than just using the actual rocket ship emoji.[22]

All of us scrolling our Twitter feeds had absolutely no clue what was happening. The only information we had was a cryptic tweet from Marc Stein and a few other posts of players trying to get to the weirdly quiet Jordan any way they could. Reports revealed that the Clippers contingent had convened at Jordan's house and had essentially locked him in dressed in full Wonder Woman outfits[23] to convince him that the team he'd been flirting with all summer was wrong for him, and there was love back home all along. To the outside world this appeared to be a hostage situation. Griffin posted pictures of the door being barricaded along with a tent he claimed he had set up in the backyard anticipating the summit being an overnight ordeal.

As with any story being told through Twitter, there was likely quite a bit of fabrication in the events that took place that evening, mixed in with a bit of truth. Take away any of the pictures posted, and emojis on Twitter that made the evening seem like

---

22 To this day I am curious if Paul Pierce knows how to use his own Twitter account or if someone has to help him.

23 This happened during The OC Christmas episode, Summer dressed up as Wonder Woman as her gift to Seth and to seduce him. See? I told you we would get back to it.

#M🏀MENTS

a high-speed chase combined with a straight up kidnapping that made the day so confusing and we still have the truth of the matter. The Clippers had locked DeAndre Jordan in his house. No one came, and no one left. Not even Fegan, his agent, was allowed in. Jordan was ignoring Cuban and Parsons' attempts to reach out and before long, everyone following along that day knew what had happened. Jordan had changed his mind and was about to spurn his agreement with Dallas to re-sign with the Clippers.

For the time being, DeAndre Jordan and the Clippers were just like Seth and Summer, they belonged together. Despite Anna/Chandler Parsons giving them literally everything they could have wanted, sometimes love finds a way to work out its differences and forgive. What was a clearly messed up and somewhat unprofessional situation, got even uglier thanks to Twitter. Without this medium we would have received reports that evening that DeAndre had changed his mind and was going back to the Clippers. There would have been a few articles over the next few days, and the world would move on. Instead it was a 12-hour digital circus complete with an actual hostage situation, and the Mavericks were made fools very publicly. It's difficult to bring up DeAndre Jordan, free agency, the Mavericks, Clippers, Mark Cuban, or anyone involved without this night coming up. This was essentially the final Rose Ceremony on The Bachelor, except with the runner up being locked out of the final venue and finding out they were getting dumped through a series of emojis. How does anyone recover from that?

After DeAndre made his decision, he fired his agent later that summer, somewhat indicating that Fegan had pressured him into committing to good buddy Mark Cuban and the Mavericks. The Mavs were left scrambling, considering the rest of the league had essentially committed to each other thinking Jordan was going to Dallas. The Mavericks had also quit trying to negotiate with any other player thinking they had Jordan locked in. Seth and Summer eventually got married and raised a rabbit named Pancakes. The Clippers continued to be good but stuck in the league's "middle ground."[24]

What would have happened if DeAndre had a few less days to think about all this? The NBA took action and shortened the moratorium by a few days in response to the debacle. Other fallout is difficult to pinpoint. Of all the stories in this book this is the least recent and was really the first time the #NBATwitter community set itself on fire reacting to tiny bits of information without context. Going forward, the NBA has leaned into this practice, and the community that follows along for the ride accepts

---

24 Over the next few seasons the Clippers would have an overall record of 194-134, never made it past the first round of the playoffs and traded everyone of consequence except DJ, who left them again for Dallas eventually in 2018.

#M●MENTS

the unwritten rules. If anything of any sort of substance happens, pour kerosene on it, watch it burn, and figure everything out afterward.

What Does Conduct Detrimental to the Team, Really Mean?

W E CAN ASSUME THREE THINGS TO BE unequivocally true. 1. We can assume that the NBA as it stands today delivers both on and off the court, many times in unnecessarily dramatic ways. 2. We can assume that, since its inception, the NBA has always been unnecessarily dramatic; however, we did not have the resources or the platform to learn about such daily occurring madness. 3. We know that sometimes the most ridiculous questions are the ones that MUST be asked and generally Twitter is the only place where such questions are demanded. This chapter will be split into two separate sections. The first being the moment that inspired it and that actually happened, and the second is a fictional #NBATwitter history.

"Conduct Detrimental to the Team"[25] suspensions

---

25   Henceforth known as CDT.

are not new to the league nor are they going anywhere anytime soon. Teams can pretty much suspend players for whatever they like, and a CDT suspension is usually because of a violation of some sort of rule set by the team or coaches. Missed curfew, late to practice, maybe a failed drug test, things like that. But what if it's not always that simple?

On March 1st, 2018 Cleveland's JR Smith was suspended one game for CDT. This wasn't exactly surprising as JR has always been a bit of a problem child throughout his career. He has been suspended and fined for just about everything ranging from brawls during games, repeated drug offenses, and my personal favorite, a weird habit he used to have of purposefully untying opponents shoes during games.[26] So when it was announced that he was suspended it wasn't that surprising, especially when Coach Ty Lue said "something happened at the pregame shootaround." Everyone just assumed he was late or maybe was just acting like an ass or something.

The beauty of Twitter is that with any event, of any sort of substance, information is out there immediately. Any thought or piece of information, true or untrue, can be thrown out into the Twitterverse immediately. There are reporters around NBA teams almost all the time. We can assume they have always asked questions like "Yo why isn't JR playing

---

26   This is right up there with when Ron Artest yanked Paul Pierce's shorts down while the ball was in play.

tonight?" They've always been given the "official" answer: CDT. Having been around basketball all my life, I can tell you that the real story isn't super hard to find, you just have to ask the right people and they will spill it. Twitter provides a tool to share that information without any real barriers or hurdles to publish it.[27] Brian Windhorst of ESPN was the one to break this story. JR Smith was suspended for one game for....wait for it.....THROWING A BOWL OF SOUP AT ASSISTANT COACH DAMON JONES. This of course led to many, many questions.

Where the hell did JR get soup right after shootaround? Did he bring a thermos or something? What kind of soup was it?[28] Was it hot? Where did this happen, on the court, locker room, WHERE? Was it a splash type motion where you fling the soup out of the bowl or did he throw the whole bowl at him as well?[29] What did Damon Jones do to deserve to have soup thrown at him? Is this the first time that JR has thrown his lunch at someone?

JR Smith's aerial assault (I'm assuming it was more of an overhand lob rather than an underhand scoop action. Many questions still remain) with water-based

---

27 Think editors for a newspaper or a producer for a local news station or something. First, the story is greatly delayed compared to Twitter, and second Twitter doesn't ask questions like "Eh, is this something we should really dish on?"

28 Thanks to the investigative powers of Twitter we know it was chicken tortilla.

29 Again Twitter, the whole bowl.

meals causes us to question what else has been hidden from us over years. So, here's what we are going to do. We are going to work backwards in time starting in March 2006 (Twitter's launch date) all the way back to March 1995 (which is plenty)[30] and imagine that I was around the team that day, heard what actually happened from a ballboy or something, and fired off a Tweet. I am going to examine each, and every suspension labeled as "conduct detrimental to the team" and make assumptions about what each player was suspended for. The rules are pretty simple. 1. The player must have been suspended by his team, and not the league. 2. There must not be a reason for the suspension listed. That's it, those are the only rules.[31] Some of these will be easy, some a little more off the wall but, come on, the real-world example we have here is a player throwing a bowl of soup at a coach. Literally anything is on the table. Or being hurled off it by JR Smith.

February 24th, 2006: Salim Stoudamire suspended by the Hawks for two games for CDT- This one BARELY missed being reported via Twitter. Salim is a cousin of former Portland Trail Blazer great[32] Damon Stoudamire, who was famously arrested on

---

30 It's also the furthest recorded I could find before records started getting weird and convoluted.

31 Fair warning, I'm going to break these rules.

32 Damon was a childhood hero for me. You'll catch no Mighty Mouse slander from here.

separate occasions for hotboxing his yellow Hummer and trying to sneak weed through airport security in tinfoil. Gut reaction is something drug related, but that's WAY too easy. My guess is that Salim is a big speed skating fan and decided to attend the Winter Olympics in Turin to witness Apolo Anton Ohno win his second gold medal in the short track. The team declined to give him permission to attend, but basketball is just what Salim does for a living, speed skating has his heart. Luckily the two-game suspension was sort of a favor as his flight home from Italy kept getting canceled. Thanks United.

December 1st, 2005: Vashon Lenard suspended by the Nuggets for one game for CDT- Literally the day before the Nuggets suspended Vashon, they suspended coach George Karl two games for openly criticizing officiating. In a closed-door meeting Vashon requested that team management suspend Karl for the rest of the season. He claimed his request was because he felt coach Karl was setting a poor example for the team's younger players by not respecting referees. However, after a little research the team discovered that Lenard figured he might get to play more with Karl out of the picture. The Nuggets being both extremely confused and angry Vashon would ask for such a thing, knowing they had to suspend him, but they were also impressed that he stood up for what he believed in and respected his hustle, so they made it for only one game.

May 3rd, 2005: Kwame Brown suspended by the Wizards for the remainder of the playoffs-[33]Kwame Brown, one of the biggest draft busts in league history, was left behind when the Wizards were in the middle of their playoff series with Chicago. Then President Ernie Grunfeld[34] gave the reason as "philosophical differences." At the time of the suspension Kwame Brown was just 21 and having grown up a basketball phenom and being drafted at 19 years old meant that sadly much of his childhood was stolen. Long flights in the hectic NBA schedule allowed time to finally get around to exploring the Harry Potter series, something he shared in common with Ernie Grunfeld. They both watched *Harry Potter and the Goblet of Fire* on a team flight and Kwame shared that he was disappointed that S.P.E.W.[35] was not included in the movies as it was in the books. Grunfeld dismissed Kwame's opinion saying that S.P.E.W. was not important to the overall outcome of the story. Kwame who was a big-time supporter of both Hermione and Dobby the house elf argued that Dobby was a very important character and that S.P.E.W. gave Hermione depth as a character. They fought for the entire flight and once they landed Grunfeld decided that Kwame's opinions were not that of a man who could be trusted

---

33   Not listed as CDT but I'm counting it.

34   Ernie Grunfeld knows a thing or two about draft busts.

35   Society for the Promotion of Elfish Welfare, which was Hermione's political group which fought to get house elf's more rights. Really important stuff.

#M⬤MENTS

and banished him from the team. Kwame was initially to spend his suspension in a cupboard under the stairs of the Wizards practice facility, but the NBA players union stepped in and disallowed it.

January 30th, 2005: Rafer "Skip to my Lou" Alston suspended by the Raptors for two games for CDT- Rafer's suspension was for an incident at Raptors practice. Based on this chapter's general content, my immediate thought was what kind of lunch time food Rafer threw at which member of the Raptors basketball operations department. However, based on his history in the And1 Mixtape tour, I was able to surmise that he was suspended two games for constantly showing off his impressive ball handling ability during drills and for refusing to NOT throw bounce passes off Matt Bonner's face. Matt Bonner is a Canadian treasure and shall not be treated in such a way!

January 28th, 2005: Darius Miles[36] suspended by the Trail Blazers for two games for CDT- Our first Jail Blazers reference! There are actually some details to this moment. Miles was suspended after a confrontation with Blazers coach Maurice Cheeks during a film session. Apparently, it was serious enough that

---

36 This was not long after The Perfect Score came out, a movie about a group of high school students that stole the answers to the SAT test. At this time, I'd like to recognize the fact that Darius Miles starred in a movie with both Chris Evans and Scarlett Johansson. Put that in your pub trivia quiver for appropriate usage.

Cheeks considered resigning after the incident. The "Jail Blazers" were mostly really bad individuals but a really good team. This incident was toward the end of the "Jail Blazers" era when they were trying to clean things up, so right around then the Blazers were mostly just a bad team. My guess is that this one is fairly straightforward, at this point in the season; the Blazers had lost 13 of the past 16 games, including a game on January 26th at home to the Mavericks. A game which Miles played a lot but poorly. A guy who didn't play a lot in that game was rookie Sebastian Telfair[37]. So, I'm going to say that Miles got into a shouting match with Cheeks for not playing Telfair more, and demanding that instead of film from the loss to the Mavericks, the team pre-screen the upcoming documentary film *Through the Fire* so they could educate themselves of Telfair's talents.

October 12th, 2004: Qyntel Woods suspended by the Trail Blazers- I'm breaking my own rule, because we know the reason for this suspension, but I want to point out some of the crazy shit Qyntel Woods used to do as a member of the Jail Blazers. In March 2003, he was pulled over in Portland and instead of presenting a driver's license he provided his rookie

---

37 Speaking of Jail Blazers, Telfair was once found with a loaded handgun on one of the Blazers team flights. He insisted that the gun belonged to his girlfriend and that he grabbed the wrong suitcase before the road trip. At the time of writing this he is appealing a three-and-a-half-year prison sentence for gun and drug charges.

trading card as identification. For this particular suspension the team shut him down while they investigated his involvement in bankrolling a dog fighting ring. #NBATwitter would have had a field day with both of these moments.

February 21st, 2004: Lamond Murray suspended by the Raptors for one game for CDT- Lamond threw a punch at his coach for saying that his cousin, fellow NBA player Tracy Murray looked better in a Raptors jersey.

January 5th, 2004: Loren Woods suspended by the Heat for one game for CDT- Woods was also suspended multiple times in college[38] and this was something he sorely missed. Loren Woods was suspended for entering the University of Miami locker room and attempting to suit up for one of their games after having a rough week with the Heat.

December 8th, 2003: Stephen Jackson suspended by the Hawks one game for CDT- This was pre-Malice in the Palace Stephen Jackson, but here's what you need to know about Stak...this man is fucking crazy in the best way possible. He's easily one of the top five players I wish Twitter had existed for during his playing career.[39] Even now retired from the NBA

---

38 And by multiple teams. Wake Forest for "basketball reasons" and Arizona for NCAA rules violations.

39 The Top-Five is as follows: 1. Charles Barkley 2. Michael Jordan 3. Stephen Jackson 4. Ron Artest(No not Metta World Peace.

this man is picking fights on Instagram with Andrew Wiggins and his brother. How many players can be suspended for 30 games then AFTER the suspension be required to take anger management courses? Steven Jackson, that's who. Since this is only a one game suspension there's no way he fought a teammate, but it was definitely some kind of physical altercation. I'm guessing a bus driver or maybe a flight attendant.

November 28th, 2003: Greg Ostertag suspended by the Jazz for one game for CDT- While doing research for this chapter, I noticed Greg Ostertag was actually suspended quite a bit by the Jazz and it really seems like he and Coach Jerry Sloan kind of hated each other. Since this can't just be something like..." didn't show up for practice" the only clear explanation is that Ostertag blew off a team dinner at Sloan's house and insulted his wife's specialty brisket.

April 21st, 2003: DeShawn Stevenson suspended by the Jazz for CDT- This suspension didn't have a number of games listed, but it was right before the playoffs and it was definitely because of a fight with Jerry Sloan...who unless you're John Stockton or Karl Malone must have been a tough guy to get along with as with the aforementioned Ostertag. Stevenson has a

---

I'm talking RON ARTEST the dude who asked for time off from the Bulls to record a rap album and who also applied for a job at Best Buy to get an employee discount, THAT guy had something to say) 5. The 00-01 season Rasheed Wallace.

pretty well-known beef with one LeBron James[40] and was quite vocal about it early in his career. Stevenson here during a shootaround stated blasphemous things like "I wish LeBron was in the Western Conference so we could meet in the playoffs." Jerry Sloan believed LeBron to be the second coming of Michael Jordan, whom he still sees in his nightmares, and would not accept such behavior or mentality, and promptly sent Stevenson home where his hatred of LeBron only grew.

April 12th, 2003: Danny Fortson suspended by the Warriors for four games for CDT- In 2006 while with the Sonics, Fortson was suspended for two games for throwing a chair after a game against the Kings. What wasn't known at the time was this was actually an example of a lesson learned by Fortson. Notice the relatively small amount of time he was suspended along with the relatively small piece of furniture he threw. That is because on April 12th, 2003 Danny Fortson attempted to launch a couch across the locker room. Yes, attempted. Danny Fortson may be a large man, but couches are tough to move by

---

40   It's one of the better NBA player rivalries that no one really knows about mainly based on the difference in caliber of the two players. In the near future of this suspension Stevenson called LeBron "overrated" which led to LeBron responding with "That's like Jay-Z saying something bad about Soulija Boy. There's no comparison". From here Stevenson had Soulija Boy sit courtside at one of their games against one another, and LeBron had Jay-Z write a diss song to troll Stevenson. Truly remarkable stuff.

yourself. Still, the damage he intended on causing drew a four-game suspension from the organization.

March 27th, 2003: Joseph Forte suspended by the Sonics for one game for CDT- I'm going to let you in on a not so secret little secret. The NBA is full of conspiracy theories.[41] Joe Forte was a bit of a clairvoyant, often being vocal that the team was about to be sold and moved somewhere far away from the Pacific Northwest. Forte prophesied that they would draft one of the best players in league history, only to have the franchise ripped from them and fans would be forced to watch from afar. Joe Forte knew too much and was suspended for a game in an attempt to silence him. The Sonics did not make the playoffs that season. From this point until the end of their season Joseph Forte only played in two games for a total of about 13 minutes. A mere seven months later before the start of the next NBA season, Joseph Forte was waived by the Seattle SuperSonics. In 2007 they drafted one of the best players in league history (Kevin Durant) and in 2008 they moved to Oklahoma City never to return again to Seattle. Joseph

---

41   Here are a few of my favorites. Michael Jordan didn't retire to play baseball; he was banned from the league because of a gambling habit. (Since rebuffed by The Last Dance) The Morris Twins, Markieff and Marcus have traded places multiple times and played as the other one when it best suited them. Michael Jordan's "Flu Game" was actually an attempt by Utah fans to poison him. (Pretty much confirmed in The Last Dance) In the 2014 Finals the Spurs turned off the air conditioning on purpose to make LeBron James cramp up.

Forte, after being released, would never play in the NBA again.[42]

March 11th, 2003: Bonzi Wells suspended by the Trail Blazers for one game for CDT- Less than a month after this, Portland's Zach Randolph was fined $100,000 and suspended two games for punching teammate Ruben Patterson and shattering his face. Wells this season only shot 29% from three-point range, and this was at the height of the Jail Blazers era. There is an extremely good chance that Bonzi Wells threw a sucker punch at a stationary teammate and missed.

February 26th, 2003: Ron Artest suspended by the Pacers for one game for CDT- We've already touched a little bit on the antics of Ron Artest. We know a few things about Ron Ron here. He enjoys time off during the season, and he appreciates receiving items at a discount price. Ron Artest was suspended for doing one of those "eat this entire giant item in one sitting and receive your meal for free" and showing up to practice unfit to play in their next game. On the 25th they were in Boston, so sadly it was probably something like, a 100oz bowl of clam chowder.

January 3rd, 2003: John Amaechi suspended by the Jazz for one game for CDT- In yet another clash with Jerry Sloan, Amaechi refused to re-enter the

---

42 I don't want to hear any "SonicsGate" bullshit. This is how everything happened.

previous game unless Sloan allowed him to run point guard instead of John Stockton.

November 29th, 2002: Ricky Davis suspended by the Cavaliers for two games for CDT- Breaking the rule here again, as it's known that Davis was suspended for an on-court shouting match with a teammate during a game. But I thought now would be a great time to mention the time Ricky Davis in a blowout win against Utah, had 26 points, 12 assists and 9 rebounds. In an attempt to get his first career triple-double once the ball was inbounded to him Davis shot on the wrong hoop to gather the rebound in hopes for the final stat he needed to get his milestone. Little did he know this did not count under NBA rules, but it counted in all our hearts as a wonderful moment in NBA history.

February 2nd, 2002: Marc Jackson suspended by the Warriors for two games for CDT- Some details are known about this one as well. Before his suspension Jackson was suspended for criticizing team management for turning down a trade that would have sent him to Phoenix. This actually goes a little further than just being unhappy in Golden State. Jackson's relationship with the team was strained from the beginning as this was well before the Warriors were a competent NBA franchise. Despite having been in the league for 10 years prior to when they drafted him in 1997 the Warriors THOUGHT they were getting then Pacers point guard Mark Jackson and instead ended up with Marc Jackson the power forward. Three weeks later Marc with a C was traded to Minnesota.

March 23rd, 2001: Michael Smith suspended by the Wizards for two games for CDT- By this time Michael Jordan was a minority owner of the Wizards as well as President of Basketball Operations. Always a competitor, Smith beat Jordan in a supposedly casual one-on-one game after practice. After his defeat Jordan told Smith "I should cut your ass" to which Smith responded that Jordan was washed up and couldn't play in the league any longer. This resulted in Smith's suspension and Jordan's eventual return to the league from his second retirement to prove a point.

December 28th, 2000: John Starks suspended by the Jazz[43] for one game for CDT- Starks who earlier in his career played in New York was not fond of sleepy life in Utah where most places close at 9pm. While at Applebee's one night, Starks sat at the bar and ordered a double whiskey coke. When told he had to order food in order to have alcohol, he placed a frustrated order of cheese sticks so he could get his beverage. He was then told that it was state policy that they could not serve him a double and could only serve him a single shot in his drink. So, Starks orders two single whiskey cokes, at first insisting the

---

43   Count me surprised that Utah appears on this list fairly often.

second was for someone else, and dumps them both into one glass. He was then kicked out of Applebee's and along with his suspension is no longer welcome at that restaurant chain.

November 15th, 1999: Isaiah "JR" Rider suspended by the Hawks for one game for CDT- I should point out that even though this is Rider's first time appearing on this list...that doesn't mean that he wasn't suspended frequently, just that most of the time they were by the league or there was a well-known reason for the suspension. I think it's a little too on the nose here that Rider would go by "JR" considering the inspiration of this chapter. So, in JR Smith fashion, Isaiah Rider was suspended for sneaking a fifth of Hennessy onto the bench during a game.

April 3rd, 1998: Oliver Miller suspended by the Raptors for one game for CDT- Oliver Miller was 6' 9" and throughout his career would flirt with weighing 400 pounds. In this case he was suspended for insisting on carrying the 5' 10"[44] Damon Stoudamire into practices like a small baby.

March 9th, 1997: Dontonio Wingfield suspended by the Trail Blazers for one game for CDT- This happened on the same day that our boy Isaiah Rider was under investigation for assaulting employees of the team's charter aircraft. Rider wanted them to

---

44   More like 5' 8".

get an entirely different plane and fly him, alone, to Phoenix for their next game. They wouldn't do it and he went ballistic. Wingfield was suspended the same day, so my inclination is that he was the "fall guy" for Rider in this incident. However, little known fact about Dontonio Wingfield, he has a culinary degree! What really happened, was he prepared a lovely meal for the team before their flight consisting of Cornish game hen and roasted seasonal vegetables[45]. Little did Wingfield know, Arvydas Sabonis hated Cornish game hens. Team management just couldn't let this transgression slide.

January 28th, 1997: Chris Gatling suspended by the Mavericks for one game for CDT- Chris Gatling is a wonderful scam artist. He and a friend created a fake "coat check"[46] at Mavericks games. Chris would always leave a ticket for his buddy Sean, who would post up near the entrance and tell fans he was the coat check service for a mere $8. Once he had coats and money in hand, he would walk the arena and hang said coats in random locations throughout the venue and walk out with roughly two thousand dollars per night. He and Chris would split this evenly. When the Mavs found out they had no choice but to

---

45 A very Portland style dish indeed.

46 I actually think a coat check at NBA arenas is a FANTASTIC idea. Holla at your boy Adam Silver. **Patent Pending** The Blazers have one, but it's outside of the arena.

suspend him for a game.[47] Who would fall for this coat check scam? Anyone dumb enough to own a coat in Dallas that's who.

January 24th, 1997: Chris Morris suspended by the Jazz for one game for CDT- In clear violation of team rules Chris Morris would routinely play Chumbawamba in the locker room before and after home games. Eventually enough is enough.

October 31st, 1996: Jeff McInnis suspended by the Nuggets for CDT- Note the date on this, as back in the 90s the NBA season typically started around Halloween. Denver's season opener was on November 1st, meaning McInnis didn't even make it to the regular season before he was placed on the shelf. The suspension was lifted on November 8th, so he missed the first four games, and this had to be something fairly serious. Southern born and bred, McInnis insisted on stocking the locker room fridges with Southern Comfort and Sweet Tea, as opposed to Colorado's own Coors Light. Team owners were both shocked and deeply offended and decided they needed time away from the player to gather their thoughts. McInnis was sent to camp in the Coors brewery for four days and required to drink nothing but Coors Light until he was brainwashed and had no recollection of his

---

47 I don't actually think this is too far from the truth. Gatling was arrested in 2015 for being involved in an online credit card scam.

affinity for southern beverages. In fact, his first game back from suspension he did not play due to a massive hangover.

April 3rd, 1995: Latrell Sprewell suspended by the Warriors for two games for CDT- Long before he was suspended 68 games for choking out his coach during practice, and even longer before turning down a three-year $21 million dollar contact because "that wouldn't feed his children" our man Sprewell made a wager of two game checks to Chris Mullin that he could jump over a moving car while it was driving straight at him. Mullin agreed to this bet, and after practice pulled up a Chevy Suburban. Sprewell insisted that he was thinking more along the lines of a Honda Civic and refused to go through with the act thus prompting Mullin to win the bet, however Sprewell refused to pay. Team executives heard about this and suspended Sprewell, then forwarded his lost wages from the suspension to Mullin to cover the bet.

March 16th, 1995: Anthony Mason[48] suspended by the Knicks for five games for CDT- It should be pointed out that this period of time was when the NBA had a "suspension list" which essentially deactivated a player from the active roster. The minimum amount of time to be placed on this list was

---

48   As a kid I used to think it was the coolest thing in the world that Anthony Mason was ambidextrous. Now knowing basketball a whole lot better, I realize that's really just something you need to do in order to play in the NBA.

five games. So realistically Mason's transgression may have only been worth one game, but he got five by virtue of being placed on the suspended list. Mason was likely suspended for fighting Charles Oakley. He wasn't suspended for the fight itself, but rather his terrible decision of picking a fight with one of the toughest fuckers in NBA history. You don't go at Charles Oakley man. You just don't.

That's it, that's every recorded yet undisclosed conduct detrimental to the team suspension in pre-Twitter NBA history. I will wait for a few years before exploring if these details I've written here actually turn out to be correct.

The Most Improbable Night in NBA History

A DRIAN WOJNAROWSKI HAS CHANGED MY sleep schedule forever. You never know when a Woj Bomb might come, meaning if you don't have your Twitter alerts turned on you miss the news and by the time you see it an hour later, you're already behind the game. I did not grow up in an era with Woj Bombs or Twitter alerts. My one and only social media was Myspace which I would log onto once a day through dialup internet. I didn't get my first cell phone until I was a junior in high school.[49] The news cycle was slower then. In many cases you wouldn't find something out until it was in the paper the following day.[50] Believe it or not I used to read the good ol' sports section in the newspaper the following morning to see any headlines and pour over box scores, along with SportsCenter while I ate my cereal.

---

49 I still miss T9 text messaging.

50 Today I cannot even fathom constantly being a day behind with news and events.

My father was my first "breaking news" alert when it came to the NBA. He worked construction, so he was up around two or three in the morning getting ready to go to work and would usually have reruns of the previous night's SportsCenter playing in the background. There were two times from my adolescent life that something big happened, when my father knew without a shadow of a doubt that I had to see it right that very second. Moments that, if I didn't see them right then, before the papers in the morning, it would have been like I didn't see them at all. One of these moments was when Kobe Bryant scored 81 points against the Raptors[51]. However, the first moment he woke me up in the dead of night is the one I will truly never forget: The Malice in the Palace.

What was a fight between the Pacers and the Pistons after a hard foul on Ben Wallace turned into a fight between the Pacers and the Pistons'...fans. It was about six guys against about 300 guys, and the six guys won the fight. If Twitter had existed then, it would have been broken during that night[52]. Not unlike the night in January 2018 when the Clippers and Rockets faced off with each other in the locker room and turned Twitter into a feeding frenzy. These

---

51 One of my favorite things on the internet is a picture with Rajon Rondo, Vince Carter, Paul Pierce, Steven Jackson, Chauncey Billups and Jalen Rose all standing together and smiling. The caption says, "Smile if Kobe dropped 40 on you" and someone photoshopped a second smile onto Jalen Rose's face because Kobe dropped 40 on him twice.

52 Figuratively speaking of course for all your literalists out there.

#M⊘MENTS

are the top two fights in NBA history[53] and two of the most improbable stories in NBA history. Going into each of these nights, nothing could have prepared you for what would unfold a few hours later. While we know quite a bit about both evenings, it's for different reasons. The Malice in the Palace happened right in front of our eyes on the court. Everything that happened is easily confirmed and the outright absurdity on full display. The fight between the Rockets and the Clippers (which I am hereby dubbing Chris Paul's Bravest March) happened behind closed doors and out of sight. The story was largely told through Twitter, and while details are equally ridiculous as the Malice in the Palace, they got even more so thanks to Twitter's nature of turning one thing into many, many others.

Still, the question must be asked: Which of these fights, is the most improbable moment in NBA history? Two stories, one without the aid of Twitter to increase its improbability, the other with only the insanity Twitter provided. We will compare each fight through a series of categories and award a point to whichever fight wins that category. At the conclusion of the chapter we will gather the final tally and award the crown of the most improbable night in NBA history.

---

53 Consideration was also given to the fight between Larry Johnson and Alonzo Mourning which resulted in Jeff Van Gundy clinging to Mourning's leg for dear life.

Category 1: CONFIRMED PUNCHES THROWN

Malice in the Palace- This is EXTREMELY difficult to determine. I've watched the main footage from the ESPN broadcast along with a few others that have different angles and different pieces of the event no fewer than one hundred times, and I'm only confidently able to count 11 punches. The footage is very grainy in quality and it's quite chaotic, just SO many moving pieces. The easy thing to say is that infinite punches were thrown as there is really no way of knowing everything that happened in the scrum.

This whole thing started when with under a minute to go in the game Ben Wallace drove to the rim and was fouled hard by Ron Artest. Wallace went right at Artest and shoved him violently in the face/neck area sending Artest stumbling backward.[54] Both teams proceeded to go about the typical NBA form of posturing and acting like they were about to throw hands, especially Steven Jackson who was the only one to actually square his hands to his face in the classic ready to fight position. While this all was happening, Ron Artest was lying on his back on top of the scorers' table and somehow a Pistons fan walked down and threw a beer on him. This was when quite literally, all hell broke loose.

---

54 For what it's worth I am not counting this in my punch count, being that it was more of an open-handed shove than anything else.

Artest charged into the stands knowing exactly who had hit him with the beer, grabbed the fan by the back of the neck, and slammed him into the seats.[55] While Artest was being pulled away from killing this guy by about eight people, Steven Jackson, by then also in the stands and almost unobstructed, threw the first haymaker into some unsuspecting guy's jaw. That's one. The footage then zoomed out to the typical broadcast view and then back into where the scrum was happening. All the while, announcer Mike Breen was losing his mind as he called this fight play by play just as he would normal game action. We then can make out Steven Jackson being held down by a ton of people, but he still managed to take his second swipe at a fan at the bottom of the pile. That's two. Punches three and four are easily the most explosive of the bout. They're not caught on the original ESPN footage (there are other videos where it is as clear as day) but you notice Mike Breen say, "and now there's another fight in front of the Pistons bench." It's unclear how either of them got there but somehow Ron Artest was now back on the floor and squaring off with a Pistons fan on the court. Artest took one swing and knocked the fan to the ground and then was quickly pulled away by teammates and coaches. As the fan was being helped up, Jermaine O'Neal

---

55   Also, not an actual punch.

came from LITERALLY NOWHERE at full sprint and knocked the fan out cold.[56]

Punches five through eight aren't really visible until the replay of the brawl. The footage is a slightly different angle from the moments after Artest and Jackson bounded into the seats. Jackson had just taken his first swing, and in this view you can see Artest being pulled down a few rows and a fan in a blue windbreaker had him in a fairly weak headlock from behind.[57] Artest took three quick short hooks to the side of his head then broke free, spun around, and sort of back-handed the fan with his left, then punched him flush with his right. That's eight.

Part of the reason Artest was able to break free from the man in the blue windbreaker, was that teammate Fred Jones was attempting to pull him off and be one of the few Good Samaritans of the evening. A Pistons fan in a grey pullover took exception and steamrolled the unsuspecting Jones to the ground. The Pistons' fan landed three punches before Jones somehow squirted away from the bottom of the pile.[58] That's 11. I'm SURE there were more that I was unable

---

56 If the man that was knocked on his ass by not one, but two NBA All-Stars happens to be reading this ...I would like to buy you an adult beverage good sir. If anyone deserves it, it's you.

57 Bush league move, but honestly, probably the only way he was going to get a punch to connect.

58 Fred Jones was one of the few Pacers players who wasn't suspended in the aftermath.

to make out or see clearly, but for the purposes of this exercise the official count is 11 punches thrown.

Chris Paul's Bravest March- Here's the thing about this particular fight, almost no one saw exactly what happened unless you were actually there for the show. That said, all corroborations of the incident indicate that zero punches were actually thrown. The closest we got was an on-court scuffle that resulted in two ejections from the game and Trevor Ariza trying to fight Blake Griffin and Austin Rivers after the game, but nothing physical actually ever came to fruition.

This category goes to the Malice in the Palace.

Category 2: BEST URBAN LEGEND

Malice in the Palace- I could tell you that the Central Division rival Chicago Bulls had sleeper cells in the stands to provoke players into doing something stupid in hopes of getting them suspended or that Ron Artest had taken a bunch of speed before the game and seeing monsters prompted his leap into the seats. Truth of the matter, there really is no urban legend to speak of with the Malice in the Palace. However, there was an interesting individual present during that night. One of the referees working the game was Tim Donaghy, who in 2007 resigned from his position during an FBI investigation into whether he gambled on games he was working during the previous two seasons[59] and

---

59   Which would include this game.

made calls that would impact the point spread of those games. Although not confirmed, it is possible that the Malice in the Palace was a game that Donaghy had money on and thus attempted to influence the outcome. Who knows? Perhaps if Donaghy had made one more call or one less comment, tempers wouldn't have flared and none of this would have ever happened.

Chris Paul's Bravest March- As noted previously the NBA has a history of urban legends and conspiracy theories. The 1985 draft lottery was rigged so that the Knicks could select Patrick Ewing. Delonte West had sex with LeBron's mom possibly leading to LeBron leaving Cleveland for the Miami Heat. Michael Jordan "retired" because of gambling problem. There are a ton. Ranking near the top of the charts are the secrets that lie in the depths of the Staples Center. The story, as told on Twitter, involves the Rockets making their way through a secret tunnel and into a back entrance of the Clippers locker room to challenge Austin Rivers[60] and Blake Griffin to a fight. The news of the altercation, of course, announced by Adrian Wojnarowski, was that Rockets players had forced their way into the Clippers locker room using a "back entry." Twitter of course turned this into a valiant expedition led by former Clippers player Chris

---

60　One of the absolute funniest things about this evening was that Austin Rivers didn't even play in the game yet pissed off the Rockets so much that they charged through a back door in their locker room to fight him.

Paul, who having made Staples Center his home in previous seasons, would be aware of the existence of said secret tunnel. Reports followed the next day that there is no "secret" tunnel, and that it is more of a well-known hallway that connects both locker rooms. In Woj's defense he did not report it as a secret tunnel either, that's just what Twitter turned it into. But what if we did actually stumble onto something here? What if there really is a secret tunnel? If this was really a well-known hallway wouldn't someone have heard of it before this?[61] Really what is even the purpose of having a hallway connecting the home team and visitor locker rooms in the first place?[62] Isn't it possible that Chris Paul, being pissed off at his former team would know of a way to go confront them?

Regardless of reports stating it doesn't exist[63] the secret tunnel in the Staples Center is one of the greatest urban legends in NBA history, thus adding to the lore of Chris Paul's Greatest March. They get the point for this category.

---

61   I'm thinking mostly of when Rick Fox and Bobby Jackson came to blows in 2002 or when Chris Childs hit Kobe Bryant twice before Kobe even knew what happened. How did these guys not hit the secret tunnel after the game?

62   Also, does this walkway connect to the Lakers locker room as well?

63   In order to be a great urban legend, many need to doubt its existence altogether.

Category 3: BEST "IN MOMENT REACTIONS"

Malice in the Palace-There are a couple that could be considered here. Here are the nominees.

- Austin Croshere standing in the middle of the court just staring at the chaos knowing he can't leave because the tunnels to the locker rooms are blocked with fighting.

- Bill Walton being literally speechless.

Reactions are best when one is not involved with the actual moment. Austin Croshere, while playing in the game, did nothing during the fight. He didn't go into the stands, he didn't throw any punches, and he didn't pull a Fred Jones and try to pull fans off a teammate. He literally just stood there politely and waited for it to finish so he could go into the locker room. Croshere's presence yet absence from the melee earns him consideration for the best in moment reaction.

However, the most shocking thing about this night is that if you've never seen the footage until today you would have never guessed that Bill Walton was also on the call. He is mostly silent throughout aside from saying "this is a disgrace" and something a bit indecipherable about this being one of the uglier nights in league history. For a man who seems to be always talking, it's jarring to hear him say almost nothing.

Chris Paul's Bravest March- Par for the course during

this moment is that we never actually witnessed any sort of in moment reaction. The entire story was told via Twitter, so we have choices of either something we were told that happened via Twitter reporting or a reaction from an outsider using Twitter to publish their reaction to what was unfolding. Here are the nominees.

- A Clippers staff member opening the front door of the locker room and immediately slamming it in either Clint Capela OR Tarik Black's face.

- This wonderful tweet from Seerat Sohi of Yahoo Sports. "Congratulations to Chris Paul for actually leading a team somewhere."

From the sounds of it, once the Rockets breached the Clippers locker room via the secret tunnel, they didn't actually get much further than that. As much as Austin Rivers might have deserved to get his ass kicked, Trevor Ariza and Gerald Green never got the chance to do that. Team security stopped anything from actually happening, making the door being shut in a player's face really the only physical reaction worth mentioning other than the march through the secret back tunnel in the first place. However, please refer to what I have affectionately named this fight, Chris Paul's Bravest March.

As the only reaction to actually influence the name of its fight, Chris Paul's Bravest March wins this round.

Category 4: THE FALLOUT
OF EACH FIGHT

Malice in the Palace- Let's start with the suspensions, of which there were 146 total games lost via suspension from this one incident. Ron Artest alone was suspended for 86 total games.[64] Steven Jackson was suspended for 30 games[65], Jermaine O'Neal 15 games, Ben Wallace six games[66], Anthony Johnson five games, and Reggie Miller, Chauncey Billups, Derrick Coleman and Elden Campbell each got one game.

The Pacers started the 2004 NBA season with a 7-2 overall record[67] and went 37-36 the rest of the way, good for sixth place in the Eastern Conference. This meant being on the same side of the playoff bracket as...the defending NBA Champion Detroit Pistons, but without reigning NBA Defensive Player of the Year Ron Artest. The Pacers were eliminated in the Conference Semifinals by the Pistons, who went to lose in the NBA Finals to the San Antonio Spurs. In the Eastern Conference that year only Miami and Detroit finished with more than 50 wins. Before the Malice in the Palace, Indiana was on pace for 63 wins

---

64 The remainder of the regular season, 76 games plus 13 more in the playoffs.

65 Honestly, this seems like a huge bargain considering the damage he did. However, he did have to attend anger management after the completion of the suspension.

66 For the initial shove of Artest.

67 Including the result of the game against the Pistons that was never actually finished.

until suspensions sent their season off the rails. It wouldn't be egregious to say that the Malice in the Palace cost the Pacers a chance at the NBA Title.

Chris Paul's Bravest March- The only players to receive suspensions were Trevor Ariza and Gerald Green who got two games apiece. Ultimately the aftermath of the incident was fairly inconsequential, but we did learn a few things. Among those being that Austin Rivers might be the most hated player in the NBA and at any given time during the season there may or may not be an altercation happening just on the other side of a trap door on the rear side of the Staples Center home locker room. That's not nothing folks.

Malice in the Palace is the answer here, as the outcome altered an entire NBA season and potentially who won the Championship that year. This means we are tied 2-2, only one way to settle this.

Category 5: BEST USE OF A TROJAN HORSE

Malice in the Palace- There are a couple of people that could be considered a potential Trojan horse. Ron Artest could be considered a Trojan horse in the most basic way; he literally led the attack and the charge into the stands. Being that the actual Trojan horse was filled with soldiers to attack unassuming victims, this isn't too far from reality. We could also say that the fan that threw a beer on Artest was the Trojan horse because he is responsible for lighting the fire that started the fight. Really though, there wasn't a Trojan horse during the Malice in the Palace. There was no real distraction or "trap," it was just a bloodbath right from the start.

Chris Paul's Bravest March- Here is the biggest argument in defense of the existence of secret tunnels lining the Staples Center. It was reported during the madness of the evening that Rockets player Clint Capela[68] knocked on the FRONT door of the Clippers locker room and that the door was shut in his face. The following day another report attempted to correct the Twitter wildfire and insist that the knock on the door, and Rockets players coming into the Clippers locker room from the back were not simultaneous. Having spent much of my life within a basketball locker room I can tell you a few things. 1. If anyone on the team was about to fight someone, the whole team is going whether they intend on throwing hands or not.[69] 2. It's really, really hard for something like this to be going on without everyone being aware of what's happening.

If we are to assume that the knock on the door was after Rockets players had already entered the

---

68 As noted earlier, the next day the report was corrected that it was Tarik Black that knocked on the door and not Capela. Important point though is that a Rockets player knocked on the front door of the locker room.

69 For example, see the Malice in the Palace, in which just about every player other than Austin Croshere was involved in some way, shape or form, and even Austin Croshere was still present.

Clippers locker room, then Clint Capela[70] either didn't know what was happening or chose not to be involved. I'm telling you neither of those things happened. The entrance was meant to be a SURPRISE, meaning the knock on the door was supposed to be a distraction because no one was expecting anyone to use the back door secret tunnel entrance because it's a secret and no one knows about it, except someone who used to play for the Clippers, like Chris Paul.

Chris Paul literally sent a Trojan horse as a distraction so that he could lead the rest of his team on a secret tunnel assault of Austin Rivers. That's why they win this category thus making Chris Paul's Bravest March the most improbable moment in NBA history, despite no one actually seeing what happened.

Twitter is so much fun.

---

70   Or Tarik Black.

# #

Agents of Change

TWITTER HAS GIVEN PLAYERS A PLATFORM TO speak their minds as openly as they wish. Many take to Twitter to pump out 280 character bursts to promote causes important to them, draw awareness to social issues, praise their buddies, and throw not so subtle shade at their enemies. Twitter has produced wholesome moments like the pure delight of Giannis Antetokounmpo when he tasted a smoothie for the first time. It also brought slightly less wholesome moments, like right after Dennis Rodman created a Twitter account, we found out that he owns a few horses and has broken his penis multiple times.[71]

Until this point, we have explored Twitter moments that didn't really change anything. Moments that would have happened with or without Twitter, but their impact was certainly aided by the platform. This section is about the events that took place as a direct result of Twitter or its influence.

---

71 It's remarkable we have made it this far into the book and we haven't talked about Dennis Rodman's penis yet.

Eric Bledsoe and the no good, very bad, terrible Phoenix Suns-

NBA players demanding trades isn't really anything new or notable. However, the way they are requesting them has become more theatrical after Eric Bledsoe seemed to demand a trade from the Suns but insisted, he was at a hair salon. The 2017 Phoenix Suns were bad, bad enough that they were outscored by a total of 92 points over their first three games of the season.[72] One day after losing to the Clippers by a final score of 130-88[73] Bledsoe indicated that he'd had enough of this, with a simple Twitter post of "I don't wanna be here." Bledsoe, who recognized the Suns standing in the league that season, reportedly had privately requested a trade prior to the start of the season. The Suns refused and entered the year with a team that not only had already imploded upon itself but was now also carrying an unhappy point guard. When asked about his tweet, Bledsoe insisted that he was at a hair salon with his wife and simply wanted to leave.[74] Everyone could see that this was a fairly obvious demand for a trade, and Bledsoe was shut down by the Suns until 16 days later when they agreed to trade Bledsoe to Milwaukee. Somehow, Eric

---

72 The worst scoring margin over three games in NBA history at that point.

73 The Suns second game in a row of allowing 130 points.

74 Literally just hours later the Suns announced they had fired Head Coach Earl Watson. It's difficult to determine if Watson had posted anything on Twitter that might have led to this.

#M●MENTS

Bledsoe managed to work his way from probably one of the worst teams in the history of the NBA to a promising team in the Eastern Conference by simply tweeting five out of context words.

Since then other players have gotten creative displaying their dissatisfaction with their current situation to force a trade. Kawhi Leonard only played nine games during the 17-18 season rehabbing a mysterious quad injury before being traded from the Spurs to the Raptors. Jimmy Butler led a group of rag-tag third-string players and dominated a Timberwolves practice while simultaneously cursing out team management and verbally berating other players.[75] While no player has *explicitly* demanded a trade through Twitter there is one that has come close: Anthony Davis.

Rich Paul, who represents Davis, informed Adrian Wojnarowski that Davis wanted to be traded and had no interest in signing a contract extension with his current team (New Orleans). Woj reported this through his Twitter account and the NBA determined that Davis violated a league rule that restricts players from using their agents to publicly request trades. So, in a six-degrees of separation kind of way, Anthony Davis used Twitter to demand a trade.[76] Players will

75 There was an interview not too long after this practice where Butler claims he only shot the ball one time which is not at ALL how I pictured this going down.

76 He was actually fined $50,000 for this. Then late in the year he made #NBATwitter waves while wearing a shirt to the final

continue to use Twitter and to come up with strange ways to ask for a trade. However, it will be difficult for anyone to put in as little effort as Bledsoe did in order to get his wish. The power of Twitter folks.

Chandler Parsons eviscerated by the Blazers-

During the summer of 2016 due to a gigantic new television deal, NBA teams saw their annual salary cap number spike to $94 million, up $24 million from the previous season.[77] Instantly every team in the league had money to burn on guys like Chandler Parsons, who was offered a four-year maximum-contract for a total of $94 million guaranteed by the Portland Trail Blazers. Parsons left his meeting with the Blazers having not agreed to the proposed contract and then held court with the Memphis Grizzlies, with whom he soon agreed to and signed a contract identical to the one Portland offered to him. Naturally, Parsons isn't very well liked in Portland by Blazers fans who believe he spurned the team. The Trail Blazers though, would get the last laugh in January 2017.

During a contest between the two teams in

---

game of the Pelicans season that said "That's All Folks" in Looney Tunes style writing. Davis would later say that the shirt meant nothing and that he doesn't even pick out what clothes he is wearing himself and that they are laid out for him.

77 The salary cap only typically increases somewhere in the $1-3 million range per year. Biggest ever yearly increase before the summer of 2016 was $8 million.

Portland, Parsons came off a screen from Marc Gasol and fired up what appeared to be a fairly routine 3-point shot only to come up about six inches short of the basket for an airball. The Trail Blazers official Twitter account pounced on the opportunity to make sure his airball was ceremoniously remembered forever on #NBATwitter, posting a video of the shot along with the caption:

> *"To be fair, the NBA 3-pt line is really, really far away from the basket."*

Being active on Twitter like most NBA players, Parsons responded to the post wishing the Blazers luck in the draft lottery that summer.[78] CJ McCollum (who is one of the more low key trash talkers in the league,[79] and I mean this as a compliment) rushed to respond to Parsons in the best way possible, claiming that Portland had already won the lottery by not having signed Parsons.

McCollum turned out to be correct in more ways than one, as the Parsons signing never panned out

---

78   Funny thing about this is that the Blazers and Grizzlies both made the playoffs that year thus avoiding the draft lottery that Parsons had referred to. The Blazers finished 8th in the Western Conference and the Grizzlies 7th place. So, the Grizzlies were the higher seed yet picked 17th in the draft while the Blazers pick landed at 19. Oh, also the Blazers didn't own their first round pick this year as they traded it to Denver for Arron Afflalo. So, per usual, joke's on Parsons again.

79   Just ask Evan Founier. McCollum once during a contest blew Fournier kisses while telling him that he was soft like a crepe.

for Memphis. Of the 246 games the Grizzlies played while Parsons was on the roster, he only played in 95 (or about 38%) due to various injuries, ailments, and clashes with team management. In these 95 games he only scored 7.2 points per game (his career average is 12.8). The Grizzlies made the playoffs during his first year with the club and missed the following two years, while the Blazers made the playoffs in each of those three seasons.

The real story from this interaction was the response from the NBA itself. The reaction from the Trail Blazers team account and CJ McCollum belittling Parsons was enough to prompt a memo from the league to all 30 NBA teams. The memo was to "warn of the inappropriate use of social media." I believe this would have been the league's first comments of any kind regarding Twitter since 2009 when Charlie Villanueva sent a tweet during halftime of a game. That moment prompted the league to create guidelines for social media, even though at the time they were quite minimal. They didn't think to update anything until 2017. For that CJ McCollum and the Trail Blazers Twitter staff achieved legendary status for having a rule changed due to their actions.[80]

---

80   There are TONS of rule changes influenced by players regarding contracts and on-court behavior etc. The other entrants into the Rule Change Hall of Fame for more fun things are; Allen Iverson who prompted the league to change its dress code for inactive players, Darryl Dawkins who caused the league to change the material that backboards are made from because he kept breaking them while he dunked, and Vince Carter who caused the league to ban players from listening to their own music with headphones during warmups.

#M●MENTS

Which Brooks? -

It would not be hyperbole to state that Adrian Wojn-arowski is the most trusted man in all of the NBA. The respected source for breaking news regarding trades, contract negotiations, and injuries is normally two-steps ahead of just about everyone else. There are even some that believe that until Woj posts it on Twitter, it hasn't actually happened yet, or that it's a fake report. So, what happens when a "Woj Bomb" is actually incorrect? On a cold December night in 2018, the clairvoyant that #NBATwitter leans on as a pillar of truth reported that there had been a three-team trade agreed to between the Suns, Grizzlies, and Wizards that would eventually go off the rails.

Woj reported the trade as the Wizards receiving Trevor Ariza from the Suns, the Grizzlies getting Kelly Oubre from the Wizards, and the Suns acquiring Austin Rivers from the Wizards and "two role players" from the Grizzlies. A subsequent tweet revealed that those players were Wayne Seldon and Dillon Brooks. Here's where it gets tricky. The Grizzlies at that point in time had two players on the roster with the last name Brooks: Dillon and Mar-Shon. Almost immediately Woj corrected himself and said that MarShon would actually be the "Brooks" included in the swap.

The tweets that would follow from Woj began to confuse and bewilder the situation. What was initially three separate teams working harmoniously with one another quickly turned into one of the more incompetent moments three professional basketball teams have ever had. It was revealed that the Suns and the Grizzlies had never actually talked to each other regarding this trade, and that they were using the Wizards to communicate all information between each partner in the trade. Meaning the first time the Grizzlies learned they were shipping Dillion Brooks to Phoenix was on Twitter. Consequently, the Suns also learned from Twitter they were actually receiving MarShon. The Grizzlies insisted they were trading MarShon while the Suns believed they would be receiving Dillion, all while the Wizards, who were supposed to be orchestrating the whole thing, had no idea at all what was going on. There are a few important things to remember with all of this. First being that Woj is a reporter, and a damn good one at that, meaning he only was sharing the information he had received. Secondly, all three of these teams were a total train wreck during this season[81] so it's not terribly surprising that they managed to botch a potential trade due to sheer negligence.

Oddly enough a version of this trade still managed to be worked out. Phoenix would eventually send Trevor Ariza to Washington for Austin Rivers[82]

---

81 Phoenix was one year removed from the Eric Bledsoe situation, Washington's entire team hated each other, including a practice where John Wall told the Wizards GM to "go fuck himself", and Memphis was staring a full rebuild right in the face after bad signings(Chandler Parsons) and injuries to their franchise cornerstones.

82 Rivers was almost immediately released by the Suns.

and Kelly Oubre. This was almost the same trade that was agreed to previously with the exception of Memphis being left out entirely (hinting that perhaps the Grizzlies were to blame for all of this despite the Wizards apparently orchestrating it). The Grizzlies would eventually trade both Wayne Seldon and MarShon Brooks (seriously MarShon, no confusion this time) to the Chicago Bulls and Dillon Brooks while still with the team only played in six more games over the rest of the season due to injury.

While this was a wildly entertaining and humorous moment, it was also an avoidable one and likely wouldn't have happened without Twitter's influence. The quick draw nature of Twitter reporting led to this trade being leaked before any team involved had an opportunity to double check their work. Without Woj's Twitter report, there is a chance that the mistake or miscommunication never happens...or maybe the trade is completed, and MarShon Brooks reports to Phoenix because the Grizzlies were never called out.

Magic just wants to be our friend-

On April 9th, 2019 Earvin "Magic" Johnson had been President of Basketball Operations for the Los Angeles Lakers for a total of 777 days and decided he'd had just about enough of that shit. During his tenure as head honcho of the Lakers, Magic was fined twice for tampering with two seperate players

(NBA rules do not allow teams to make public comments or communicate with a player under contract for another team) and warned about tampering with a third player.[83] While they never made the playoffs during his reign in the City of Angels and won only a total of 79 games, he did manage to accomplish a few things, notably bringing LeBron James[84] to the purple and gold. Despite landing LeBron, his time in the front office will be remembered for poor personnel moves and speaking out of turn. That's exactly what happened right before tipoff of the Lakers final game of the 2019 season.

The Lakers were preparing for the season finale before catching flights to various vacation destinations when Magic decided to hold an impromptu press conference to announce his resignation from the franchise. Magic moved forward with this plan without the counsel of the team, coaches (many believed the coaching staff was going to be fired by Magic himself either after the game or the following day), or anyone involved with the team. He mentioned that team owner Jeanie Buss was not aware that he was making this announcement, and that he had not actually spoken to her about his decision. He even hinted

---

83 The players he was actually fined for were Paul George and Giannis Antetokounmpo and the player he was warned for was Ben Simmons. No other team in the league during that period of time was punished for tampering.

84 I guess an argument could be made that LeBron was heading to LA with or without Magic Johnson's influence though.

#M☻MENTS

that he was afraid of doing so and couldn't bear to do it face to face. It was an embarrassing moment for a historic and powerful franchise that appeared to now be the punchline of the entire league, let alone the warped minds of #NBATwitter. It would take months for us to learn which direction the Lakers would take upon Earvin's abrupt departure, and on the night of his monologue[85], Magic's reasoning for the decision to step down was a bit blurry to say the least. Some of the things he said though, left breadcrumbs as to what Magic Johnson was about to become.

The tampering fines and allegations hurt Magic Johnson the executive on a personal level. He was accustomed to being the entire league's quirky relative that would show up uninvited to holidays and make awkward and slightly suggestive comments. But what if I told you that all of this drama and confusion, turning his back on the franchise that gave him the name "Magic," and betraying his brother-like relationship with Jeanie Buss was so that he could tweet out box scores, what he was eating that night, and tell us about his favorite movies? Magic wanted to say whatever he wanted to whomever he wanted, and he wanted to be able to do that...on Twitter. Allow me to show my work. If #NBATwitter was a singular person, Magic Johnson would be like the first attempt at creating it that wasn't very good and you know

---

85 His press conference was a sight to behold. Lasting well over forty-five minutes and was basically just him talking until well after tipoff of the actual game.

you've got to do better on the next attempt but this one is already here, so you know, what can we do about it now? Let's just leave him alone and let him do his thing.

Magic didn't want to be accused of tampering and he was never trying to do anything wrong, he just wanted to talk with his buddies. During his exit speech Magic laid it all out on the table for anyone that wanted to pick it up. *"I thought about Dwayne Wade retiring tomorrow, and I can't even tweet it out or be there."* Of all the things he said during his final press conference as part of the Lakers[86] that was the most meaningful sentence. His Twitter account, and hanging out with his basketball buddies, was more important to him than his responsibilities with the Lakers. #NBATwitter often appears as if everyone in the world is abandoning more important things in order to tweet about the Knicks, or Robin Lopez, or the Bulls Mascot, or Kristaps Porzingis following a supermodel on Instagram. Magic Johnson is the first one to actually do that in person, and he should be celebrated for it. Since his resignation he has provided exquisite content to the NBA Twittersphere, and he is quite possibly the only person on the planet that can tweet his favorite snacks (Skinny Pop Popcorn with Sea Salt and Pepper) and it's an enjoyable moment for us all. He also has a weird way of forgetting that all of us are watching the same content, often tweeting

---

86   He said a lot.

the exact NBA game schedule like a TV Guide and exact final scores and stats for games that we all just watched. And everyone loves it.

In a way this should make us all feel good about ourselves and remember what's important in life. Magic Johnson is just like us. All he wants is to just sit back and enjoy the show while every now and then reacting to it like "Wow Steph Curry scored 37 points tonight. Unstoppable!" Bottom line, his Twitter account mattered more to him than being President of the Lakers did, which is both hilarious and relatable.

Who Is the NBA's One True Lord of Whispers?

COMMUNICATION IN *GAME OF THRONES* VAST continent of Westeros ranged anywhere from men on horseback relaying news to more metaphorical messages, such as setting a building on fire or delivering an enemy's head to a ruler. But the fastest and most powerful way to share news was to use ravens to carry important messages. The types of information presented with this format varied in terms of reliability depending on who had sent the message and what their own personal agenda was at the time. But once any new information was out, a chain of reactions would ignite chaos all over the world. Sound familiar? Westeros was pretty much just Twitter without the internet. I mean, they even used birds and Twitter's logo is a bird. How much more obvious can this be?

The absolute best at using this medium to spread

truth as well as lies was Lord Varys[87] a.k.a. "The Spider." Varys literal job was to know what was going on and to spread information using his network of "little birds"[88] which were a ton of small children that spied for him and reported what they saw. So essentially, imagine a soft-spoken bald man in a robe, that has a verified Twitter account with a million followers. Then at a daily meeting he shares what he read on Twitter and then posts some of his own shit to promote the realm's agenda and that might be just his own version of the truth.[89]

We are first introduced to Varys as he's sitting on King Robert Baratheon's small advisory council where he almost immediately shares information from his Westerosi "Twitter account" that Daenerys Targaryen had married. This piece of information was true. He then sends ravens to order the assassination of Daenerys at the instruction of the King and other members of the small council. This part is true as well. He does this by using an informant on another continent, Jorah Mormont to spread the message. We find out multiple seasons of the show later that Varys's actual loyalties were with Daenerys and not

---

87   I want to point out that we will be speaking about the television version of Varys, not the book version. Each chapter in the *Game of Thrones* books is written from the point of view of a character, Varys is not a point of view character in the books. So, you have a much better idea of what his motivations are and all the shit he is pulling from the television version.

88   More evidence that Westeros used Twitter.

89   I'm realizing that if you've never seen *Game of Thrones* this must sound insane to you.

#M🌑MENTS

whomever happened to be sitting on the throne at the time (I think he served like three separate rulers other than Daenerys) and he eventually moved on to support and advise her. So, while he might have been "tweeting" the truth at times, he had many ulterior motives. It's almost impossible to know if he shared every bit of information he knew, or if what he actually shared was true, as he had a hand in many acts of betrayal throughout the series.

Varys had much the same type of role with the Targaryen council. However, much like real life Twitter, much of the information he was receiving and passed along was really bad or extremely sensitive and shouldn't have been shared at all. As he was really the only person with any information that could be spread, because this was his only job, there was no one to cross check him. Advice that Varys provided based on information of his "little birds" led to military disaster for the Targaryens and in the end would cost him his life[90]. If this sounds at all familiar it's because it happened in the NBA as well.

Sam Hinkie joined the 76ers as their General Manager in 2013 and ushered in the method of "tanking" or methodical losing to gain assets and burn the current state of the franchise to the

---

90 People can say what they wish about the final season of *Game of Thrones*. My biggest issue was that throughout the entire series Varys acted in the shadows and was extremely careful. Only to meet his end in the second to last episode by standing on a very wide-open beach asking Jon Snow if he'd like to help him commit a very large act of treason.

ground and rebuild anew. The history of the 76ers is much like that of the Targaryen dynasty in *Game of Thrones*, decades of history and greatness[91] followed by a lengthy period of promise-filled insanity and mediocrity making Sam Hinkie like the Mad King Aerys[92]. Sam Hinkie and "The Process"[93] began with optimism, carrying out unique strategies and gaining a loyal cult following. During his reign he drafted players such as Joel Embiid and Jahlil Okafor[94] which signaled a return to prosperity all while carrying an overall record of 28-136. Despite failures, life for the 76ers was mostly positive during Hinkie's tenure, as he turned the NBA realm upside down with his new vision and methods. Along with the many losing streaks[95] while Philly's General Manager, Sam Hinkie conducted more than 80 total transactions involving

---

91   Sure, they only have one championship in the post-ABA merger era, but they have three in total, and a history of some of the most iconic players in league history.

92   Aerys' methods were to burn everyone alive. Hinkie's were to trade everyone for a second-round draft pick. Pretty much the same thing.

93   You should probably know this, but in case you don't, "The Process" was the nickname for the 76ers during Hinkie's tenure with the team. He would commonly address fans and the media asking them to "trust the process" when asked about his obscure methods for building a team.

94   He also drafted Michael Carter-Williams, who was "fine" and won Rookie of the Year. But he drafted him over say, Giannis Antetokounmpo, Steven Adams or Rudy Gobert.

95   In 2014 they came really close to breaking the NBA record for consecutive losses to start the season. League record is 18 in a row. The Process lost 17 in a row.

#M⬤MENTS

over 120 different players.[96] His methods were obscure to say the least, but Hinkie's loyal followers had players like Embiid and Okafor believing that the future was bright.

On December 8th, 2015 the 76ers hired Jerry Colangelo as a "special advisor" to the franchise. Then in April of 2016 (a day after just their 10th win of the season no less) Sam Hinkie resigned, and days later Bryan Colangelo (Jerry's son) was hired in his stead.[97] Like Aerys, Hinkie was unseated by a usurper in a somewhat unsavory fashion[98] and Colangelo was left to build off an already solid foundation. Bryan Colangelo was basically hired by the 76ers to complete "The Process" that was begun by Hinkie.

Having inherited a team that had just finished the season with a 10-72 overall record Bryan Colangelo was armed with the number one overall pick in the draft to begin his rule over the 76ers by selecting Australian point guard Ben Simmons. Despite Simmons sitting out his entire rookie season because of a broken foot, the Sixers managed to win as many games that season as they had the previous two, 28.

---

96   This does not include transactions where the same player was added to the roster and released from it multiple times, which also happened quite a bit.

97   So, to recap Jerry Colangelo was hired in a position of power, Sam Hinkie resigns, and Jerry hires HIS OWN SON to replace him. Some real *Game of Thrones* type shit indeed.

98   Yes, I'm considering being forced out by your boss's son to be on an equal level with being literally stabbed in the back by your own bodyguard.

The following year, with a healthy Ben Simmons they amassed a 52-30 overall record and finally made the playoffs, making it all the way to the Eastern Conference Semifinals before being eliminated. "The Process" appeared to be complete, and Philadelphia seemed poised for conquest.

Success had returned to the City of Brotherly Love, but there were still remnants of the team's recent past. "The Process" was still present as Hinkie's promises of a brighter future were still on the roster. With Jahlil Okafor and Joel Embiid still around, Bryan Colangelo's reign could never truly be peaceful. Both Embiid and Okafor would miss over 40 percent of the team games during the first two seasons of Colangelo's tenure (Okafor missed over half the Sixers games in that time period) and health and effort level was a constant question mark for each player. Still, they were in the playoffs and on the surface at least, the relationship between Hinkie's holdovers and Colangelo seemed to at least be amicable. That is until it got very strange, very quickly.

20 days after Philadelphia was knocked out of the playoffs, a report from Ben Detrick and "The Ringer" was published that detailed a series of obscure Twitter accounts that all seemed to have similar points of view and interests. The story, with the help of an anonymous source, revealed five separate Twitter

users that followed mostly the same accounts[99] (or similar accounts at least), interacted with the same people (mostly 76ers beat writers and anyone critical of Colangelo) and were critical of the same things (mostly Okafor, Embiid, and Hinkie).

The concept of "burner" accounts for NBA personnel was a relatively new revelation before "The Ringer" report. "Burners" are Twitter profiles used outside of your main or verified account. Less than a year prior, Kevin Durant was actually caught doing it when he replied to a tweet calling him out regarding leaving the Thunder. Durant responded from his verified Twitter account, but his message was worded strangely, as if he was talking about himself in the 3rd person. It later was revealed that he forgot to switch profiles from his actual Twitter account, to his "fake one" before defending himself. All of a sudden #NBATwitter was aware that at any time a player or team executive could be hiding in plain sight behind a "burner" account. "The Ringer" report would expose a few more of those.

In addition to a general disdain for "The Process" and those that remained, each account showed an affinity to Colangelo golden boy Ben Simmons, often expressing this by insulting Joel Embiid (who carried the nickname, "The Process") and questioning the

---

99 Twitter's algorithm is not unlike that of any normal cookie on your web browser. Based on your search history and contacts etc, it will suggest accounts for you to follow when you create an account.

player's effort, attitude, and value to the team. The strongest of these statements came after a concert in which Embiid both attended and pranced on stage shirtless. One of the accounts referenced in "The Ringer" investigation, "Eric Jr." which seemed to be the most outspoken of the mysterious little birds, said the team needed a "ladder to knock some sense into Embiid." One of the other phantom accounts in question by "The Ringer" had also been known to suggest the use of ladders being required when speaking to Embiid, mentioning things like, "if I had a ladder" or "if I could get a medium sized ladder to speak with him". The anonymous source in the report suggested that there was no way that two separate Twitter users could be using this extremely specific and unique example of needing a ladder to speak to one particular NBA player. These two accounts had to be controlled by the same person.

The most staggering and concerning thing about these Twitter accounts was how they seemed to have confidential and sensitive information about the 76ers and some of their players. The accounts were mostly inactive until February 2017, then they began to share things seemingly out of nowhere that were damaging to Process remnants Okafor and Embiid.[100] 76ers beat reporter Keith Pompey posted on Twitter about a particularly strange couple of days involving the team

---

100 They were also fairly critical of Nerlens Noel and would trade messages with just about anyone who would suggest that Colangelo wore nothing but shirts with large collars.

#M⚫MENTS

and Process holdover Okafor. "Eric Jr" appeared to be alluding to a trade situation that fell through, and pressured Pompey to question Okafor on if he had failed a physical recently, thus ruining an opportunity for Colangelo to trade him to another team. At this point in time the Sixers left Okafor behind in Philadelphia during a two-game road trip while they assessed options to send him elsewhere. At the moment it appeared as if Okafor had played his last game with the 76ers, but in an abrupt fashion he ended up rejoining the team and hanging around for another year or so before eventually being traded to Brooklyn. Additionally, the account sent a tweet to Embiid directly, asking him to explain why he hid a knee injury from the team. Colangelo took some heat for letting Embiid play in a game against Houston. After that game the injury was revealed and would eventually end Embiid's season and require surgery. These blatant call outs seemed baseless and a bit out of context. While acting like an angry fan, the accusations were quite specific and would have been things that few people outside of Colangelo would know about.

February 2017 had a few more damning examples linking Colangelo to the accounts. One in particular indicates that one of the Twitter users, and Colangelo, were both attending the same game involving the 76ers minor league affiliate.[101] This is when "Eric Jr" began making some of the same mistakes that

---

101 I use the term "minor league" because the time this game took place was when the league was called the NBDL. It has since

would end up dooming Varys, by communicating in the open. He stopped operating in the shadows and began to reveal his location, mistakenly sharing that "Eric Jr" and Colangelo were both in attendance at a game that only 2,062 people were at.[102] Another post directed at Gabrielle Union indicated that the Twitter user sat near her and Dwayne Wade at the Olympics. At the time Colangelo was working with the Team USA Olympic team. It seemed highly unlikely that literally anyone other than Colangelo could be the person behind the "little birds."

Detrick approached the Sixers about the phantom Twitter accounts, after which Colangelo in a somewhat non-Varys like function, actually admitted that one of them was his, but that he just used it to follow the industry and never posted from it. He denied any knowledge of the other accounts. Afterward a few of the accounts in question were either deleted or switched to private accounts, meaning only followers of those users could see posts made by them. The account Colangelo claimed belonged to him was not the "Eric Jr" account, nor did it explain any of the other three accounts. Needless to say, "The Ringer" report sparked plenty of outrage and shock from those inside the Sixers organization, Joel Embiid in particular who had been the target for criticism by most of the accounts. His response was to mainly

---

changed to the "G-League" The Sixers affiliate was also called The 87ers and they have since been renamed The Blue Coats.

102 Also want to point out that one of my former players, James Webb III, also played in this game.

#M●MENTS

tweet directly at a few of the "burner" accounts as if they were in fact Colangelo, calling him out that he was not as smart or as good at his job as his predecessor, Sam Hinkie. Other Sixers players and league sources (Adrian Wojnarowski) expressed shock and disbelief that the story and the rumors could be true. No one within the league seemed to believe that a high ranking NBA executive would be that brazen and reckless, and potentially place their job in that sort of jeopardy. However, #NBATwitter users did not tend to agree and started digging for their own details, believing there was no possible way Bryan Colangelo wasn't involved with these accounts. They would discover that it wasn't Colangelo, but it was someone quite close to him.

Independent investigations by both the 76ers, and #NBATwitter confirmed that Colangelo's wife was responsible for three of the burner accounts. She would confess in an interview during the 76ers investigation, but #NBATwitter users would out her by using the feature to reset a password. By attempting to log-in to a few of the accounts in question they were able to surmise that the owners of three of the accounts all had a phone number that ended with the same numbers as Colangelo's wife. In the end Colangelo would be forced to resign from the 76ers and met his end in much the same way Varys had; by being betrayed by someone he trusted, operating in the open, and by openly inflaming those who helped bring him into a position of power.

The Basedgods Curse

THE USE OF THE WORD "CURSE" IN SPORTS IS used more as an embellishment rather than a statement of fact, and this also holds true for the NBA. "Curse" is defined by Merriam-Webster as "a prayer or invocation for harm or injury to come upon one" or "a solemn utterance intended to invoke a supernatural power to inflict harm or punishment on someone or something." Popular belief is that Portland Trail Blazer centers are cursed. Allegedly, this began when the team drafted a big man named Sam Bowie from the University of Kentucky one spot before some guy named Michael Jordan. Bowie spent much of his career sidelined due to injury and had more screws surgically implanted into his leg (16 in total[103]) then he played years in the league (10) while Jordan went on

---

103 Bowie had three screws placed into his leg during his third season in Portland. Two of those screws didn't hold and they had to place three more screws to fix it. The following year he broke his leg again which led to 10 additional screws being permanently implanted into his shin. This led to Bowie missing the next two seasons altogether. In all, Bowie only played in 63 total games with Portland.

to, well we all know that story. Portland would continue to have injury troubles in the future with other star players, Greg Oden and Brandon Roy being the most notable of them. Anytime there is an injury in Portland the "C"[104] word eventually surfaces, and we wonder, at least for a day or two, if there is something larger at play than just a string of bad luck. However as far as we know, there was never an invocation of harm.

Slightly closer to actually being cursed would be the Phoenix Suns, whose fans claim they are doomed to decades of bad luck due to the "curse of the coin flip." In 1969, the Suns and the Milwaukie Bucks were tied for the worst record in the league that season, and it was determined that a coin flip would be used to see which team received the first overall pick in the upcoming draft. The Suns lost the coin flip meaning the Bucks were able to draft Lew Alcindor[105] of UCLA. Phoenix drafted Neal Walk who by all standards had a fine NBA career, playing eight seasons with a career average of just over 12 points per game. For comparison sake, Kareem is the all-time leading scorer in league history and won six championships. What's not known about the night of the coin flip is if there was a vindictive sorcerer that bewitched the coin used or if there was some incantation used to place a spell on the coin. We do know that the city of Phoenix and Suns fans as a whole

104 Not that one you assholes.

105 He didn't begin going by Kareem Abdul-Jabbar until 1971.

#M●MENTS

made the call of which side of the coin to choose in the flip (heads), as the franchise ran a poll to determine if they would call heads or tails thus altering their franchise's history forever.[106] While there may or may not have been a "supernatural power" at work, the punishment aspect of the Suns bad luck still remains missing, meaning it's not really a curse right?

Enter Brandon Christopher McCartney, better known by his rap moniker "Lil B." The Bay Area musical artist can best be described as eclectic with a style ranging somewhere between rap and indie folk music, and he just might be one of the most interesting people ever. McCartney has not only authored and published a book[107] that led to a guest lecture at NYU, he has also given motivational speeches at universities like MIT all while referring to himself in the first and sometimes fourth or even fifth person. Lil B has over 1.3 million followers on Twitter and has used his online presence to create a virtual cult following that has progressed his music career to a point of strange underground popularity. Imagine *Fight Club* except everyone is allowed to talk about *Fight Club*. The most interesting aspect of this man though? He claims to have an alter ego called The BasedGod that routinely puts hexes on NBA players and teams via Twitter as well as bestowing blessings to those who

---

106 I seriously hope there's some Suns fan that voted tails sitting here today like "I FUCKING TOLD YOU."

107 It's actually pretty interesting. It's written like the author is emailing or text messaging the reader.

pay homage to the deity that he believes himself to be. It's not as crazy as it sounds, The BasedGod's Curse at the moment of writing this anyway, is undefeated and his divine intervention has been guiding league outcomes since 2011.

In 2011 NBA fans, unless already part of the Lil B cult following, were not yet aware of the supernatural powers The BasedGod possesses. I know this may seem confusing, you are probably asking yourself "aren't Lil B and The BasedGod the same person?" The answer to that question is yes, but also kind of no. There are times where Brandon McCartney will refer to himself as The BasedGod and we will receive information from him firsthand. There are others in which McCartney refers to The BasedGod as another person entirely in a completely different space that he speaks to from time to time. When that happens, we receive The BasedGod's message secondhand from the words of Lil B. Sometimes it is indecipherable which personality we are getting, which makes following him on Twitter a bit of a roller coaster. While Lil B himself is actually a very positive person, The BasedGod is more of an aggressive protector, and vindictive personality of sorts that Lil B will summon in times of need. This is where the story of The BasedGod's Curse begins when Oklahoma City Thunder forward Kevin

Durant[108] posted a tweet that insulted Lil B's musical talent and questioned his overall relevance.

Lil B was minding his own business, probably preparing for his eventual tryout with the Warriors G-League team (this actually happened) when Kevin Durant virtually assaulted him from long range. In an interview well after Durant's tweet, Lil B explained that he reached out to Durant with an offering. Play him one-on-one and if he lost, Lil B would stop making music and retire. NBA players are challenged to play against others all the time[109] so at that moment there was really no reason for Durant to take the challenge seriously, just another wannabe looking for his chance to shine. That's when an actual musician (Lil B) that's actually somewhat well-known went on Twitter as his ALTER EGO (The BasedGod) and cursed Kevin Durant, saying he would never win a title after disrespecting Lil B. The BasedGod had awoken from his slumber to unleash his fury.

Now of course, Kevin Durant being under a curse from a supposed Twitter sorcerer did not raise

---

108 It's wild how much of this book is about Kevin Durant. I'm just now realizing it.

109 Brain Scalabrine was called out quite a bit during his career. So much so that with the help of a local radio show he actually accepted challenges and played four different people one-on-one, all of which he beat VERY easily. Another fun one is when Dwight Howard accepted a challenge from a young fan during a rain delay (the roof to the arena was leaking) during one of his games when he was with the Rockets. He not only dunked on the kid but swatted one of his shots into the stands.

anyone's eyebrows at the time, and no one even really thought about it again until a little over a year later on June 21st, 2012. That day was Game 5 of the NBA Finals between the eventual Champion Miami Heat featuring at the time the unprecedented super team of LeBron James, Dwayne Wade, and Chris Bosh against...you guessed it, Kevin Durant and the Oklahoma City Thunder. The Thunder were victorious at home in Game 1. Durant led all scorers with 36 points and Miami Coach Erik Spoelstra made the odd decision to not start Chris Bosh[110]. Teams that win Game 1 at home in a best-of-seven series end up winning the series 86% of the time. The odd thing about this particular season[111] is that in 2012 the NBA Finals was still played in a 2-3-2 format rather than the now customary 2-2-1-1-1 format at the time of writing. That means despite having "home court advantage" over Miami, after dropping Game 2 they were tasked with three straight games on the road against one of the most formidable teams ever assembled. The Heat won all three in Miami and the rest is history.

No one could really question Durant and the Thunder; they faced an improbable task. They were less experienced and going up against a team that was

---

110 Bosh came off the bench and wasn't great, despite playing 33 minutes he did nothing noticeable. No reason was ever given for him coming off the bench in Game 1 but he started the next four and Miami won all of those, so I don't know, you figure it out.

111 Other than it being a lockout year anyway in which only a 66-game schedule was played and the season didn't start until December.

#M⬤MENTS

specifically built to dominate the NBA Finals. There should be no shame in that. Then Brandon McCartney went on Twitter and reminded us all that this was his doing and that punishment had been served. A mere 12 minutes before Game 5 of the Finals ended, what appeared to be Lil B and not The BasedGod chose positivity over anger and lifted his curse upon Durant and the Thunder, claiming that they were both now free to win future games. However, in this instance, the damage was done and Durant was left to pick up the pieces and try again.

During the offseason the Thunder shuffled their roster, mainly trading away James Harden to the Houston Rockets moments before the start of the next season; however, they remained in contention all the way until 2016. Things took a weird turn again for Durant and the Thunder in 2014 when Durant was in the middle of the best season of his career taking home both the scoring title[112] and the MVP. The BasedGod forgot any positivity he held toward Durant and reapplied the curse to him and the Thunder.[113] Lil B again offered Durant a chance to avoid the hex, simply asking for a quick game of 21 when the Thunder were in town, again Durant ignored the olive branch. Oklahoma City lost to San Antonio in the Western Conference Finals in what was likely their

---

112 He had a 32 point per game average.

113 It's slightly convoluted as to what Lil B's reasoning was this time, but something really pissed him off. In addition to the curse, he also released a new song called "Fuck KD".

best chance to win the title after the Harden trade.[114] The 2014-15 season was the worst of Durant's career as he played in just 27 games dealing with a litany of injuries including two separate foot surgeries to deal with, a Jones fracture in his right foot, an ankle injury, and a sprained big toe. Durant was officially shut down in March of that season after his second foot surgery and the Thunder missed the playoffs. The BasedGod's curse appeared to be at the height of its powers, ready to vanquish Lil B's enemies for eternity. The only doubt came in the 2016 Western Conference Finals between Durant and the Thunder and the reigning Champion Golden State Warriors.

Durant, healthy and at full strength, brought the Thunder right into the lions' den and appeared poised to slaughter the beast. Up 3-1 over the Warriors in a best-of-seven series, it appeared all but over as only nine teams had ever come back from that deficit in league history. The BasedGods curse seemed to have lost its way, until Brandon McCartney again jumped on his Twitter page to remind us that this was all part of the plan. What do all instances of The BasedGod's curse infecting Kevin Durant have in common? The BasedGod waits until Durant is THIS close (makes motion with hands like one does in this type of

---

114 This was the final year of LeBron's Heat teams but prior to the Warriors becoming a full-fledged juggernaut. San Antonio beat Miami in the Finals, so it stands to reason that the Thunder would have had a great chance to do so as well if they could have gotten by the Spurs.

situation) to reaching the apex of his career, before sweeping the rug out from under him. He lets Durant get close enough to smell greatness only to snuff it out in the most painful way possible. Losing in the NBA Finals or having an MVP season only to be followed by a season that he couldn't stay on the court, this is the type of physical and psychological warfare that would have kept a lesser man from even tempting fate again. Kevin Durant is not a lesser man. Durant was positioned to serve poetic justice to a lyricist that had tormented him far too long, by beating[115] Lil B's favorite team. The BasedGod would not allow Kevin Durant to have his day. Before Thanos there was The BasedGod, and he too was inevitable.

What we need to remember at this moment is that Lil B and The BasedGod are the same person, but they are also not at all the same person. Lil B is a very positive and outgoing individual that mostly promotes togetherness and warmth. The BasedGod is a reclusive and all-powerful clairvoyant that speaks through Lil B. On May 14, 2016 Lil B posted on Twitter that he was going to ask The BasedGod about the Warriors and to send blessings to the team. This was two days before Game 1. Then, right before tip-off of Game 1 (a game that the Warriors would take) Lil B headed back to Twitter to announce that The

---

115 Beating them pretty badly as a matter of fact. The Thunder won Game 3 by 28 points and Game 4 by 24 points.

BasedGod had responded to his request.[116] According to The BasedGod ``the Thunder will not be beating the Warriors in the playoff series, Durant is still cursed." Four days after that, the Thunder had taken a 2-1 lead, and the ever positive Lil B showed he had some of his own agency separate of The BasedGod, claiming that Durant fighting through the curse and being so close to breaking it is "a beautiful thing to see" showing for the first time that perhaps Lil B is more friend than foe.

Maybe there was a small chance that he wanted the curse to be finished as well. The Thunder now leading the series 3-1 had The BasedGod's curse looking to be a bit of a sham, or at the very least that the spell had lost some of its juice. That's the thing about curses though, they are tough to break. By May 28th the Warriors had come all the way back to even the series at three games apiece setting up a winner take all for a trip to the NBA Finals. Lil B again jumped on Twitter praising the nobility and the powerful truth of The BasedGod's curse. Oklahoma City lost in Game 7 by a final score of 96-88, by far the lowest scoring game of the series. The seemingly improbable had happened, and before the champagne had even been uncorked in the home locker room, we were reminded of who was responsible for what

---

116 This is why this is such a great story. Lil B has to make requests of his own alter ego and then is stuck with a two-day waiting period for an actual response. I don't care what anyone says, this is amazing.

we had just witnessed. Lil B let us all know that The BasedGod only speaks truth and passed respect to anyone that still believed in the curse with the Warriors down 3-1 in the series.

Life happens quickly in the NBA. Numerous times in a relatively short period Kevin Durant found himself near the pinnacle of basketball immortality only to be left in search of answers over and over again. The ways that failure found Durant seem almost inexplicable, as if he had snatched defeat from the jaws of victory. The BasedGod had a stranglehold on Kevin Durant's career, and the only way out of it was to pay tribute to the man who appeared to be responsible for multiple seasons falling off the tracks. On July 4th, 2016, just over a month after Oklahoma City's collapse in the Western Conference Finals, unrestricted free agent Kevin Durant chose to sign with the Golden State Warriors. Lil B's favorite team now had a brand-new weapon, and this pleased The BasedGod enough to lift the curse once and for all.

With the dark cloud of the curse now a thing of the past, the Warriors and Kevin Durant would win the next two NBA titles with Durant being the NBA Finals MVP both times.[117] Kevin Durant was finally free to live a life of basketball happiness, and all it

---

117 There can be an argument made that Steph Curry should have won both years instead of Durant. 2018 at the very least, Curry had a similar series as Durant and was equally deserving.

took was to show a Twitter rapper a little attention.[118] Kevin Durant; however, is far from the only player whose soul has belonged to The BasedGod for some period of time, as the curse also found its way to former teammate James Harden.

With Durant mostly injured in 2015, Lil B set his attention to what he perceived as another slight. Unlike Durant, who was originally cursed for insulting Lil B, Harden caught the ire of McCartney by imitating him without permission. Beginning in the 2015 playoffs Harden would celebrate by using something called "the cooking dance," a movement in which he would cup his right hand and flick his left wrist over the top of it, almost as if he was eating an imaginary bowl of cereal. This is a celebration that Lil B claims he created, and he merely asked Harden for an explanation, threatening The BasedGod's curse if proper credit was not given. Harden ignored the warning much in the same way that Durant had, even going as far to say that he had never heard of Lil B, and the curse was activated.

The curse would show itself to the world at the worst possible time for Harden, during the Western Conference Finals against the Warriors.[119] Already down 2-0 in the series, the Rockets lost (Game 3)

---

118 And to sign with possibly the best team ever. That's a different argument.

119 Lil B is the most powerful sports fan on the planet. If I could cast spells on teams and players going against my favorite teams, I would need an Excel sheet to keep track of everyone I had cursed.

by 35 points[120] and lost the series 4-1. James Harden would shoot just 36% from the field in the aftermath of the curse, including just 2-11 in the decisive Game 5. During that game he also set a playoff record for most turnovers in a game with 12.[121] Lil B was actually in attendance for Game 5 to bear witness to Harden's record-setting performance, further giving support that Harden was under the influence of supernatural forces. The curse would remain in place into the following season, despite Lil B publicly thinking about asking The BasedGod to remove the curse under the premise that setting a record for turnovers in a playoff game was punishment enough. The request; however, was either never made or it was denied. During the second game of the following season, the Rockets were blown out (perhaps coincidentally they played the Warriors) in a game that Harden only shot 4-18 from the field and 1-10 from three-point range. Lil B reminded everyone with a Twitter post that Harden's performance wasn't just early season struggles, and in fact he was still cursed for refusing to give credit for his use of the "cooking" celebration dance.

On June 4th, 2017 Lil B appeared on an episode of ESPN's First Take during a live broadcast

---

120 Kevin Durant's jersey number for most of his career. Coincidence?

121 Although he is tied with many other players, Harden also has the number two and three spots on the playoff single game turnovers list.

and proclaimed that he was lifting the curse from Harden[122]. During the slightly more than two-year period of being under McCartney's grasp, Harden's individual numbers flourished (he averaged 29 points per game, the highest of his career at the time) but the Rockets as a whole were trapped in the NBA's feared middle ground. They carried an overall record of 93-68 and never made it past the second round of the playoffs. Their performances before the curse was lifted led the team to trade about half of their roster to the Clippers for Chris Paul in an attempt to make a run at a title. Harden from this point forward also refrained from using Lil B's dance as a celebration, he now does a move in which he pretends to have a bloody nose.

All of these things aside, the takeaway should be that the NBA community was now finally giving Brandon McCartney the one thing he truly desired. Recognition. The BasedGods curses were born out of being slighted. Durant questioned the musical prowess of Lil B, and James Harden failed to pay homage to the inspiration for a celebration. After the seemingly inconceivable failures of two of the league's best players showed the true power of The Based-Gods curse, the entire world would finally begin to take notice for good. Even individual NBA teams (the Hawks) were now reaching out to him begging

---

122 In this interview he was dressed like a woman from Downton Abbey.

#M⬤MENTS

to be spared. The deity that watches over the NBA demands respect, but damnation is not invoked without cause. Lil B is eternally optimistic and claims that all teams and players are automatically blessed by The BasedGod unless blessings are not deserved. Since lifting Harden's curse in 2017, The BasedGod has publicly invoked more blessings than he has curses, and mostly for teams as a whole[123]. To this point no player has been given a public individual blessing, but no player has been cursed since 2017 either. We are in an unprecedented time of peace and all it took was a little love.[124]

---

123 Currently the Warriors, Celtics, Trail Blazers, Timberwolves, Sixers, Kings and Knicks carry blessings. While the Nuggets carry a "warning" of a curse for being upset about not being on Lil B's initial list of blessed teams.

124 Just in case....PLEASE BLESS ME BASEDGOD.

#

The #NBATwitter
Moment of the Decade

W E'VE COVERED A LOT IN THIS BOOK. WE'VE
explored curses. We've covered teenage television dramas and how they correspond to the Wild
West nature NBA free agency. We've talked about
Game of Thrones characters using smartphones.
We've covered some of the greatest moments in
#NBATwitter history, but which one is the greatest
of these great moments? What is the best moment of
the past decade?

Any moment from any of the previous sections of
this book could be considered the greatest moment
by some fans, but if they were in fact the greatest
moment they would be here in this section. It could
be the moment where Magic Johnson made his NBA
Finals prediction in 2014.[125] It could be the time
Kevin Durant was watching The History Channel in

---

125 Magic once claimed that the only way either the Spurs or the
Heat don't win the title was if those teams don't actually make
it to the NBA Finals.

a nightclub.[126] It could be when the king of throwing Twitter insults, Joel Embiid shared his opinion of American politics.[127] All of those are great, but none of them lasted for an entire season. None of them became a theme for one team's entire year, created merchandise opportunities, or became talking points that went with actual basketball reasons and not just social media reasons. The greatest #NBATwitter moment of the past decade, is an ode to CJ McCollum, the 2019 Portland Trail Blazers, and of course a Warriors fan named Jennifer.

The Trail Blazers began their 2018-2019 season like many teams do in the social media age, by being called out by a random fan for past failures. During August of that year, before training camp had even begun, McCollum had been making the media rounds in China and was asked a relatively simple question regarding the defending champion Golden State Warriors. The interviewer asked him what he thought about veteran players choosing to join the Warriors to "chase rings"[128] and if he believed that was

---

126 Durant wondered how anyone can actually know how the sun works since no one has actually visited it.

127 When Donald Trump won the election in 2016, Joel claimed that America had started the NBA fad of "tanking". Pretty much stating that we were going to suck for a while. Joel you were so fucking right.

128 At this point the Warriors had recently signed All-Star DeMarcus Cousins. He was recovering from a torn Achilles tendon and never produced much for them, but the addition was still significant at the time.

#M●MENTS

going to become a trend for the future of the NBA. CJ responded that he thought most players wouldn't choose that route and made it clear that he didn't approve of the tactic, saying things during the interview like "I wasn't raised that way" and "disgusting." Back home in the states, one of CJ's comments from the interview was posted on Twitter slightly out of context, prompting him to respond that his comments don't really mean anything and that he's not exactly bitter about it. Of course, Twitter users responded, one in particular caught CJ's attention. A Twitter user named Jennifer told CJ he needed to win some playoff games before he could talk shit.[129] This would light a fire under the team that hadn't been present in Portland for at least 20 years. CJ responded like any hard-working person would and responded just like you or I would respond if we had failed to do something. Sometimes a witty response isn't needed, sometimes it's better to just keep it simple. In a way that was extremely relatable yet also heroic and now iconic, CJ told Jennifer that he was trying.

Three simple words, "I'm trying Jennifer." It was a clap back that couldn't be argued with. Try for Jennifer, for Rip City, and for the NBA is exactly what CJ and the Blazers did during that season. There are four

---

129 To this point in his career CJ McCollum had actually won a few playoff games but not many playoff series. His overall playoff record before this tweet was 11-24. Four of those wins he did not play in however and the Blazers were swept out of the playoffs without a win the previous two seasons.

moments from the 2018-19 Trail Blazers season when CJ McCollum's simple message rang true. Moments when it appeared that the Blazers season was close to finished and there was no more trying for Jennifer or for anyone else, yet miraculously and improbably they pulled through.[130] Moments that seemed to define the season, that is until the next defining moment arrived.

MOMENT ONE:

The first was March 25th of that season, in a seemingly innocent game against the Nets, a mere ten games prior to the start of the playoffs. Portland had won four games in a row and was cruising toward home court advantage in the first round. The Nets were a tough team and wound up taking the game to double overtime, and there were quite a few moments that could have ended the game much earlier. Many came at the hands of D'Angelo Russell, who both missed a shot at the end of regulation that would have won it for the Nets and made a shot at the end of

---

130 I will point out right now that Damian Lillard dropping a nuclear bomb on the Thunder is not one of these four moments, but we should still talk about it for a second because it's the moment from this year that most people will remember. With the clock winding down during a tied-up Game 5 Lillard stared down Paul George about 38 feet away from the basket. There was never a doubt in his mind that he was going to shoot it from right. fucking. there. He ended the Thunder season from about a mile away, then had the audacity to wave goodbye to their bench as they left the court. Oh, and that shot gave him 50 points for the game. I dare you to find a more cold-blooded moment in all of NBA history. You can't.

the first overtime to send it to a second. The game was physical throughout and I remember looking at fans next to me and saying that this game needed to end before one of those guys got hurt. No sooner had that been said that, while battling for a rebound, Blazers big man Jusef Nurkic hit the floor. This wasn't alarming at first, any Blazers fan can tell you that Nurkic tends to get either hit in the face or knocked to the ground maybe two to three times per game. All the Nets players within the vicinity of Nurkic then ran away from him. Again, not super alarming, until you realize they weren't just running. They were in a full out sprint and covering their faces like they had just seen a ghost.

Nurkic' lower half appeared on the Moda Center big screen and the crowd groaned in a way that I'm not sure has been heard before, and I'm not sure it could be replicated. It was abundantly clear that Jusef Nurkic's leg had broken.[131] At the moment of the injury there was 2:22 remaining in the second overtime. That's how close Portland was to moving on to the next game and continuing to tune up for a long playoff run. Instead, Portland's adopted son was wheeled out of the arena leaving the team and fans alike heartbroken and recalling other eerily similar

---

131 That part doesn't need to be described. No one needs that.

moments in which a season of promise was snake bitten by a lower leg injury.[132]

The injury was devastating on multiple fronts. A) The Blazers and their fans legitimately love Nurkic. Not only had he reinvigorated the franchise after a trade from Denver, his continued growth as a player and a person cements him within Rip City forever. B) He was in the middle of a career year, paired with Damian Lillard and CJ McCollum perfectly and was the team's defensive anchor. C) The franchise has a complicated history with injuries, this particular one being more visibly gruesome and deflating than any of its predecessors. This injury was expected to doom the Trail Blazers to yet another first round exit, and another discarded "what if" season into a pile of so many others.

Instead, Portland went 7-2 over their final nine games, entered the playoffs as the number three seed and "upset" Oklahoma City in round one.[133] During the deciding Game 5, Nurkic actually returned to the Moda Center for the first time since the injury. He showed up near the Blazers bench, walking without crutches with about seven minutes to go in the game and Portland trailing by 15 points. No one had seen or

---

132 Others in the franchise's history include Bill Walton, Brandon Roy, Greg Oden and of course Sam Bowie. To a lesser extent Arvydas Sabonis as well, being that by the time he was in Portland his legs were mostly scrap metal.

133 Many pegged the Thunder as the favorite in the series despite Portland having home court advantage.

#M⬤MENTS

heard from him since he was wheeled off the court, then just as suddenly as his injury occurred, there he was. The rest of that game is well known history. What's not however is that Nurkic was wearing a shirt that mocked Thunder guard Russell Westbrook, then in a post-game interview dropped "fuck it" on live TV. This is the type of swagger and bravado that the team had carried throughout the season and now into the second round of the playoffs. The team tried, for Portland, for Nurk... and of course for Jennifer. Now according to Jennifer's comment of, "win some playoff games then talk" CJ McCollum was now allowed to speak.

MOMENTS TWO AND THREE:

Portland's opponent for round two was Denver. Jusef Nurkic's former team, the Blazers top rival[134] , and largely the team considered most likely to compete with Golden State for the Western Conference crown. Denver had bested Portland three times already that season and now had home court advantage in the playoffs. We're going to flash forward to Game 3 of the series, which at that point was knotted at one game apiece. CJ McCollum tried valiantly and led all scorers in this game with 41 points, however he was not the only hero for the Blazers, or the only one

---

134 Fans will want to say the Lakers, but this hasn't really been true since the Jail Blazers era. Others will say The Artist Formerly Known as the Sonics, but that's just not the case either. It's Denver.

that tried like hell for Jennifer. With 1:59 remaining in the game Portland forward Rodney Hood entered the game and scored seven of the Blazers' final nine points, including a three pointer with eighteen seconds left to play to put the Blazers ahead for good and seal the win. That might sound relatively routine, it was anything but. Hood's three was near the end of the fourth overtime. Prior to the 2020 season there had only been one playoff game that lasted a total of four overtimes, that was in 1953, that's how uncommon and not routine this game and Rodney Hood's moment was.[135] Even more remarkable is that Hood did not play in overtimes two and three and only played a total of twenty-three minutes.[136] He finished the game with nineteen points, seven of those in the final 1:59. That three point shot that ended up winning the game for the Blazers came after McCollum missed a jumper from about fifteen feet off the back of the rim and somehow got his own rebound. McCollum tapped it to a wide-open Hood, who pump faked his shot and let the defender fly by him before burying the shot. That was moment two. Moment three was Game 7 of the same series against Denver. This time, McCollum would get his opportunity to be the only hero.

With the series tied at three games apiece the

---

135 In total that has only happened fourteen times in NBA history. Four of those games have involved Portland.

136 For comparison sake CJ McCollum played sixty minutes.

#M⬤MENTS

Blazers entered slightly unfamiliar territory facing a seventh and final game on the road. In their franchise's history they had only played in a Game 7 three times. Once in 1990 at home against the Spurs (the franchise's only Game 7 win), again in 2000 in a loss to the Lakers on the road in the Western Conference Finals,[137] and again in 2003 in a road loss to the Mavericks.[138] Game 7 on the road was a difficult task, in fact the road team to this point had only won 27 times in league history.[139] The Blazers trailed most of the game, and no one could have faulted them if they had succumbed to the pressure. They had already overcome quite a bit to even get to that point, and even Jennifer would have had to give them credit for that.

CJ McCollum wouldn't allow it; he wasn't finished trying. With less than 5 minutes to go in the fourth quarter Damian Lillard was blocked driving to the rim, which led to a fast break layup chance for Jamal Murray. McCollum chased him down and blocked that shot into the backboard. To give you an idea of how unlikely of a moment that was, to that point in his career McCollum had averaged less than half of a blocked shot per game (.37 blocks per game to be

---

137 The famous "Kobe to Shaq" game. The Blazers blew a 15-point fourth quarter lead and 12 year old me wanted to die.

138 The Blazers almost made history. Down 0-3 in the series they stormed back to force a Game 7. If they had won, they would have been the first team to even win a series after starting down 0-3.

139 Out of 132 total games, or 20%.

exact) so for him to actually pin a shot against the backboard like he was Hakeem Olajuwon was something pretty spectacular. Portland was only up four points at that moment, and had Murray been able to convert, momentum likely would have shifted to Denver. Instead Portland never relinquished the lead. CJ McCollum finished the game with 37 points, again leading all scorers. His final points of the game came from an elbow jumper that was slightly reminiscent of Michael Jordan's shot over Bryon Russell in the 1997 NBA Finals.[140] CJ and the Blazers had done it, and by Jennifer's definition they were now allowed to speak. After the game, McCollum was asked by a reporter if he had anything that he wanted to say to Jennifer. CJ only smiled and said that he appreciated her.

MOMENT FOUR:

It doesn't actually matter what happened after the series with Denver. It doesn't matter that Portland was swept by the Warriors in the Conference Finals. It doesn't matter that their season came to a somewhat anticlimactic end compared to the storybook nature of what had taken place over the previous few months. The 18-19 Blazers were special. They overcame freak injuries to star players, withstood a type of game that had only happened once ever, and quite possibly most importantly, proved to a skeptical Twitter user

---

140 No push-off here either!

that they were no joke. CJ McCollum and the 18-19 Portland Trail Blazers achieved #NBATwitter immortality. Not only did that prove significant doubts to be incorrect, I believe this may be this may be the one and only time since Twitter's inception that an #NBATwitter moment has become an actual in person moment between two users. #NBATwitter, and the NBA at long last, meet in person.

Prior to Game 2 of the Western Conference Finals, ESPN actually had Jennifer on as a guest for a pre-game conversation, a segment in which CJ McCollum joined for a brief moment. When asked if he had anything to say to Jennifer having made it this far, all he said was, "Thank you." This is the #NBATwitter moment of the decade because it wasn't just a moment while scrolling a social media page. It became a real life moment, the two people who would have never met otherwise, shared together. It was a moment that lasted for literally an entire season, not just a fleeting moment which tends to be the nature of #NBATwitter. It was a moment that wasn't even just a moment, it was an entire team, an entire city, and an entire fanbase all coming together with one thing in mind.

Try.

Dear Mamba; 1/27/20

Author's Note: This was hard to write, but it was the only way I could figure out how to really process things in real time. At the time of writing this, I still haven't come to grips with it. These words are raw, (mostly) unedited and I don't plan on changing that. Like everyone, I did the best I could.

Dear Mamba;

ESPN was kind enough to air the final game of your career tonight. This was the second time that I have seen it. The first time I was alone in my apartment, not really understanding how truly special it was. I just knew I couldn't miss Kobe Bryant's final game.[141] I had seen you score 60 points in a game before that night, what I feel like was many times. Sure, it was pretty cool to see you do it during the final night of your career, but I wasn't surprised. I even expected it. That was a mistake. Tonight, it was different, as once

_____

141 For what it's worth at the same time the Warriors were going for the single season record of 73 wins. No one cared about that game though.

again I sat down in my empty apartment all alone to watch Kobe Bryant's final game one more time. A game that had already happened, but again I just knew I couldn't miss it.

I remember the very first time you caught my attention. I started watching basketball with Jordan and the Bulls. Just like any child that was young and didn't know better, there was a team in my own backyard. I was mostly too young to fully understand what I was really seeing. Jordan retired for the first time when I was just five years old. He didn't really honestly impact my love for the game, despite how much I say that he had in fact done that for my entire life up until this very moment. I fell in love with basketball, because of you.

I had never seen a dunk contest before the 1997 NBA Dunk Contest. I remember watching with my dad, and when you came up, he told me to make sure I watched because he thought you were pretty good. Sure enough, you did something I'd never seen before, dunking after first switching hands between your legs. "Holy shit" I remember my dad saying. My own jaw was on the floor and in my mind, I was also screaming "holy shit what was that?" Yes, at just nine years old before ever actually verbally saying "shit", my mind was exploding with the word. I was hooked. Basketball was forever embedded into my soul. Words can't really express what that means to me. Thank you for that.

A few short years later I had evolved into a

die-hard Portland Trail Blazers fan who hadn't quite begun to understand heartbreak. During the fourth quarter of the 2000 Western Conference Finals Game 7, I was sitting with my dad, already celebrating a trip to the NBA Finals. You remember that game. We were up 13 going into the fourth. That didn't matter to you. All I can remember from that game now was you throwing a lob to Shaq and shattering my dreams.

The deep rooted loathing and general fear of you as a player had fully matured by 2002. By this point you had broken my heart a few more times and I relished nothing more than any chance the Blazers had to come out with a victory against you and the Lakers. For Christmas that year, my parents got me tickets to the Blazers game against your Lakers on April 14th. It was a Sunday afternoon game and my dad and I had gotten these Bill Walton beanie baby things at the door when we came in. Scottie Pippen was ejected from the game for tossing the ball into the stands and the fans started throwing those Bill Walton dolls onto the court. I asked my dad if I could throw mine too. He leaned in and handed me his own, and said no, but to throw his instead. I still have that Bill Walton doll. The Blazers won that day, in double overtime. I'll always remember that moment with my father, and I'll always remember the first time I witnessed the Blazers beat Kobe Bryant in person.

In 2006 I knew the heartbreaks were coming. I also loved basketball more than anything, and had a deep respect and admiration for you, despite a weird hatred for all the times you tormented my favorite team. This was before Twitter or Woj Bombs. I saw scores the next day in the paper or on SportsCenter in the morning. My dad who worked construction woke me up at around three in the morning and pulled me into the living room and made me watch the replay that was currently airing of the previous night's Lakers and Raptors game. I hadn't seen it before that moment, and I know I don't need to remind you or anyone about that game. 81 points is all that needs to be said. Again, I'd never seen anything like it.

Those four moments are not only some of my favorite basketball memories, but also my favorite moments with my father. I didn't realize it until tonight, but somehow, some way you, Kobe Bean Bryant made my father and I closer. All of these feelings have been rushing into my brain uncontrollably for the last 30 hours or so. Especially seeing the heart-felt moments of you being a father the last two days.

Tonight, your final game was different. I have never cheered for the Lakers before. Tonight, I cheered every basket insanely like it was happening in real time. I clapped. I laughed. I cried. I tried to take in every little look, or piece of body language you shared with us. I absolutely lost it when the telecast flashed to your family. When Gianna was jumping up and down every time you would hit a shot. When she was blowing you kisses during your speech after the game. I lost it. I finally understood that what I had seen was truly special, in more ways than one. I didn't realize before yesterday that it was possible for me to love someone that I once thought that I hated.

I'm not sure anyone will ever have this sort of specific impact on my life again. You captivated my imagination and made me fall in love with basketball. Basketball made me closer to my dad, it's how I learned my mother would be there for me no matter what, it captivated my imagination and made me chase dreams that took me to places I never knew I would be able to go. It's in the fiber of my being and a large portion of that is because of you. Deep down I can relate with you, or at least feel like I can. We were both at one time just kids shooting socks into a basket counting down the clock in our heads. When my career in basketball was finished, it took me quite a while to feel peace with that, even now as I don't really feel that inner peace, I feel there is still something I can learn from you and finding an identity from your life after basketball. Deep down we were both nerds for the game, able to rattle off stats and key moments and thoughts like someone had surgically implanted those facts into our minds. Sometimes I feel I put people off because I love to talk about basketball so much. Something I'm sure you have experienced, or maybe not. After all, you were Kobe fucking Bryant.

Were. That's the part that still doesn't seem real. I don't know how to process exactly what I'm feeling at the moment, which is why I am writing you this letter. Weirdly enough, you've always kind of been present in my life. I just didn't know that I admired and loved you until recently. I don't expect things to change much from here, even though I know things will be different. That's ok, I won't forget. And someday, when my kids ask me why I still say your name every time I shoot a wad of paper into a trash can, I will sit them down and tell them a story about greatness, admiration, about the hardest worker and fiercest competitor I've ever witnessed, and the guy that inspired me while simultaneously tearing my heart out. Most importantly, I'll tell them about a loving husband and a father. I think I'll start with where it ended, or where it began however you want to look at it. That 60-point performance during your final game. I don't want anyone to misunderstand how special that night was the first time they saw it, like I did. Thank you, Kobe. For everything.

-TJ

#RIPKobe #RIPGianna #MambaOut
#MambaForever

Acknowledgements

Thank you to the wonderful and talented Katie Steere for taking my visions and turning them into entertaining visuals. Without your work, this book is just a bunch of words and not nearly as fun.

Thank you to Danial McCurry for your insight, ideas, and for taking my words and turning them into something that makes sense. Also thank you for correcting me every time I misspelled "Hinkie".

Thank you to Shea Serrano. We don't really know each other, but you gave me your honest opinion which provided inspiration and direction for this project. I did not really have either of those before speaking with you.

Thank you to my lovely wife Natasha, who has not read a single word of this book (I wouldn't show it to her) but supported this project for the past two years. It was also an out of context conversation with her that gave me the idea for the title #Moments.

Thank you to my brother Trey, for keeping me levelheaded through just about anything.

Thank you to everyone in my family or friend circle that I have not mentioned by name, for trying to understand what this project was about, despite it being a subject that they were not familiar with and one that I would not really tell them much about.

Thank you to my dog Taco Bella. I vent to you more than anyone and you only seem annoyed about it occasionally.

Thank you to anyone that uses Twitter. I cannot believe that shit is free.

And finally thank you to everyone at Inkwater Press, for giving me an outlet to achieve this goal, and for helping me take something silly and ridiculous from my brain and create it in the real world.

About the Author

Thane Jackson is a former college basketball coach who had the opportunity to work with a few players who made it to the NBA, including the Brooklyn Nets and the Orlando Magic. Prior to and during his tenure as a coach he earned his master's in sport and athletic administration from Gonzaga University in Spokane, Washington. He currently spends much of his time consuming as much NBA content as possible, while simultaneously interacting with Twitter. He is the author of more than 13,000 tweets, most of which are NBA related. This is his first book.